ISRAEL AND NUCLEAR WEAPONS
Present option and future strategies

ISRAEL AND NUCLEAR WEAPONS

Present option and future strategies

FUAD JABBER

1971

CHATTO & WINDUS, LONDON

for

THE INTERNATIONAL INSTITUTE
FOR STRATEGIC STUDIES

Published by
Chatto and Windus Ltd
42 William IV Street
London W.C.2

*

Clarke, Irwin and Co Ltd
Toronto

ISBN O 7011 1766 4

Printed in Great Britain by
Northumberland Press Limited
Gateshead

To my wife, Tania

CONTENTS

PREFACE

AT a time when great concern continues to be felt in many quarters about the uncertain future faced by the international community because of the threats inherent in the ever-impending prospect of nuclear diffusion, a prospect that has not been seemingly affected by the Non-Proliferation Treaty in any radical sense, there is little doubt that perhaps the most sensitive and dangerous area in this regard is the troubled Middle East. This is so in spite of the fact that the countries of that region are relatively small states endowed with limited resources and capabilities and locked in a conflict that, despite its intensity, remains essentially local in its scope and implications. Though a nuclear confrontation between China and India or a super-power clash over a nuclearized Germany might conceivably entail more serious consequences on a world-wide basis, the open-ended crisis that has characterized Arab-Israeli relations ever since the Jewish state was established in Palestine twenty-three years ago invests a nuclear Middle East with ominous possibilities, the gravity of which is compounded by the greater likelihood of their realization.

That this part of the world may be talked of in terms of locally-produced nuclear weaponry is at present exclusively due to the presence of a small but advanced nuclear set-up in Israel that carries strong military overtones regardless of its officially peaceful nature. These stem from the circumstances surrounding the programme, the nature of its main installations, the mantle of secrecy covering almost all nuclear and related activities, and the grave security problems faced by the country. Notwithstanding all arguments against the adequacy or rationality of nuclear strategies in the Arab-Israeli conflict, the one hard fact is that Israel has created and developed a military nuclear option over the years at a cost of many hundreds of millions of dollars around a facility whose main practical utility is the production of weapon-grade fissile plutonium. Whether this option was a principal objective or is incidental to a programme aimed primarily at the peaceful exploitation of atomic energy, the intimate connection that has developed

9

between the technological and scientific resources of a country and its armed capability, given the nature of modern instruments of war, makes it impossible to disregard or fail to account for the potential contributions that such resources can make to the military field. This connection exists in relation to most contemporary weaponry but nowhere is it more evident than in the area of nuclear energy applications. The whole problem of nuclear proliferation originates from the inescapable conclusion that, regardless of undertakings, agreements or safeguards, the selfsame facilities used to produce electric power and heat from the atom put their owners, simultaneously and at negligible additional cost, in possession of the explosive necessary to build weapons of mass destruction.

'The military strength of a nation,' one of the main promoters of Israel's atomic effort and former Deputy Minister of Defence has candidly pointed out, 'is measured today not only by the type and quantity of the weapons it possesses but also by its capacity to produce them in time of need—and this is particularly true of advanced weaponry. It is probably easier for intelligence services to gather information about the arms held by an adversary than it is for them to gain a correct estimate of its national potential in the field of research and in the production of existing weapons—or of new and unknown weapons.... That is probably the important area, more so that in many others, in which one nation can surprise another, and it is much simpler to conceal the means of production than the items produced.'[1] The purpose of this study is to analyse the Israeli nuclear effort, evaluate the military potential of its components, assess the magnitude of its present weapon-making capability and investigate the possible role nuclear arms may be assigned in the context of Israel's defence strategy and political objectives. Whatever new insights it may provide will be the result of a careful analysis of information gathered from published sources; no hitherto unrevealed information is included—as none was available to the author. In view of the scarcity of data in the public domain, the conclusions reached must perforce remain tentative. A more accurate assessment must await further disclosures and future developments.

Part I is devoted to a survey of the nuclear establishment in terms of its installations, research institutions, policy-making bodies and plans for future expansion. A brief history of the origins of

[1] Shimon Peres, *David's Sling* (London: Weidenfeld and Nicolson, 1970), pp. 110-11.

the programme has been constructed that reviews major developments until December 1960 when, with the disclosure of the existence of the Dimona reactor, the programme may be said to have 'come of age'. The all-important influence that the hard-core members of Israel's 'defence community' of political leaders, top military officers and chief scientists—who have remained in charge of the programme ever since its inception—are bound to have on the shaping of nuclear policy is touched upon, and the far-reaching consequences that the construction of a large nuclear desalination plant envisaged in existing projects would have for the country's ability to build up a substantial weapons stockpile is examined. In Part II, the focus is on the requirements of nuclear weapons production as they relate to the Israeli set-up and to the country's scientific, material and financial resources. Problems connected with fuel procurement and developments in the field of delivery systems are also discussed.

The third and last Part of the book consists in a short review of the ends and means of Israeli strategy as it has unfolded since 1948 in an attempt to determine to what degree and in which circumstances nuclear weapons could be conceived as an adequate instrument of Israeli policy. It is obvious that the *ability* to acquire these weapons must be accompanied by a *willingness* to do so under appropriate conditions to elicit the decision to 'go nuclear'. This willingness will in all likelihood—and perhaps more so in the Israeli case than in any other—be contingent upon a number of factors, such as the probable adversary response, the expected reaction of friends and allies, and the climate of international opinion, quite apart from vital geo-demographic, strategic and financial considerations.

It has been traditionally argued that Israel will resort to her nuclear option only as an act of desperation following a drastic—and admittedly unlikely—deterioration in the arms 'balance' that preserves her military superiority over her adversaries. This view holds that such ultimate recourse would at best serve to dissuade the Arabs from eventually attempting to overrun Israel and at worst ensure that the temple walls engulf both friend and foe in their fall were nuclear dissuasion to fail to prevent the onslaught. The present study does not try to disprove such argument, though the author entertains serious doubts regarding the rationality of basing the defence of Israel on nuclear deterrence if her neighbours become preponderant in conventional power, and the credibility of such a strategy. It does maintain that another major and much

11

more proximate incentive to acquisition of nuclear armament may be the impact that such a step would be expected by the Israeli leadership to have on the Arab-Israeli confrontation and specifically on the will of the Arab side to pursue the conflict and stand fast in its hitherto inflexible attitude towards the Zionist state.

As the events of the last quarter century have amply demonstrated, nuclear weaponry's target actually is the mind of the opponent first, and his forces or cities as a last resort. Its psychological-political power has even obviated its military use, and this power would seem particularly called for and singularly effective in the Middle East where the actual use of other than atomic weapons can never be a viable proposition. Also, the nature of the current conflict is such as to allow means and techniques of psychological pressure to exert great influence on the parties' determination of their maximum and minimum objectives and on the policies they may adopt to achieve these objectives. The lack of any amount of interaction on the popular level between the two sides prior to the initiation of the conflict—except between the Arab and Jewish communities in Palestine—and the virtually total absence of communication throughout, for instance, have resulted in the development of a somewhat distorted and magnified perception of the enemy's wickedness and the lengths to which he may go to attain his goals. Another characteristic is the great emotional as well as physical involvement of the populations on both sides of the borders in the conflict and their direct, day-to-day exposure to its ramifications and consequences.

The Israelis have been constantly mindful of these factors and have tailored their strategies accordingly. In the nuclear field itself, the statements of their spokesmen and informational policy in general have deliberately aimed at fostering a climate of uncertainty regarding the country's actual intentions and at establishing a sort of deterrent—as well as bargaining asset—based on the military option developed in the last decade. Whether this option will be eventually taken up in quest of the great 'persuasive' powers of an atomic arsenal cannot be foretold with any degree of certainty. What can be asserted with greater confidence is that the nuclear alternative will remain the subject of serious scrutiny and consideration in Israel for as long as a truly final settlement of the Palestine conflict remains unachieved, and not only as a guarantee of ultimate survival.

December 1970

PART I

The Nuclear Establishment

CHAPTER I

The Early Years

ORIGINS OF THE PROGRAMME

IN a sense, Israel has always been a nuclear country. The origins of the Israeli atomic energy establishment date from the very inception of the State in 1948. Even before the hostilities brought about by the establishment of the State on 15 May and the consequent entry of Arab forces into Palestine had ended, a scientific unit of the Research and Planning Branch in the Israeli Defence Ministry carried out a detailed survey of mineral resources in the Negev Desert,[1] discovering in the process large phosphate deposits containing uranium in proportions of 0·1—0·01 per cent.[2] After the war, the possibilities that the exploitation of atomic energy could offer as a substitute for conventional power in a country which lacked cheap sources of fuel were given careful consideration, particularly in view of the difficulties created by the need to absorb and provide work opportunities for large numbers of immigrants.

Such possibilities, moreover, seem to have been regarded with keen interest by Israel's first president, Dr Chaim Weizmann, who had been in contact with prominent nuclear, and other, scientists since the closing days of World War II[3]. Weizmann, who was himself one of the most outstanding scientists in his field—organic chemistry—has avowed the intimate connection that in his view existed between scientific achievement and the attainment of Zionist, and later Israeli, objectives. 'The reader of these memoirs' —says a revealing passage in his autobiography—'has long been aware in what an organic fashion my Zionist and scientific interests

---

[1] Ernst David Bergmann, Chairman Israel Atomic Energy Commission, Kol Yisrael Broadcast, 19 November, 1954. Foreign Broadcast Information Service *Daily Report*, 23 November, 1954. (Cited hereafter as *Bergmann Broadcast*.)

[2] Walter Eytan, Director General Israel Foreign Ministry, interview granted to *Nucleonics*, October 1955, p. 32. (Cited hereafter as *Eytan Interview*.)

[3] United Nations, General Assembly, First Committee, 9th Session, *International Cooperation in Developing the Peaceful Uses of Atomic Energy: Report of the United States of America* (A/2734, A/2738, A/C.1/L.105), 15 November, 1954. Speech by Israeli Ambassador Abba Eban, pp. 335-37. (Cited hereafter as *Eban Speech*.)

have been interwoven from my earliest years. This is ... the reflection of an objective historic condition. The question of oil, for instance, which hovers over the Zionist problem, as it does, indeed, over the entire world problem, is a scientific one. It is part of the general question of raw materials, which has been a preoccupation with me for decades, both as a scientist and as a Zionist; and it had always been my view that Palestine could be made a centre of the new scientific development which would get the world past the conflict arising from the monopolistic position of oil.'[4] This view was the fruit of the experience he had amassed in the political and diplomatic struggle for a Jewish State in Palestine that spanned the first half of this century and culminated in May, 1948. Science had in large measure provided the currency with which Weizmann had advanced his Movement's goals,[5] and now he saw in science Israel's 'mighty weapon which we must utilize with ingenuity and skill, with every means available to us. Science is that weapon, our vessel of strength and our source of defence.'[6]

Thus, the Israeli Government's early interest in nuclear power was not an isolated development or an example of remarkable perspicacity and long-range vision, but only one expression of the primordial role science and technology have been assigned in facing the development and security problems of the country. This important factor should be constantly kept in mind in any study—such as the present one—that purports to evaluate the Israeli potential in a science-related field or activity.

Within one year of Israel's establishment, the first plans for a

[4] Chaim Weizmann, *Trial and Error: the Autobiography of Chaim Weizmann* (London: East and West Library, 1950), p. 545.

[5] Weizmann's scientific achievements in the field of fermentation which had led to the development of a process for the production of acetone and synthetic rubber during World War I and of high-octane fuels during World War II earned him many friends and admirers in Britain and the United States who at several times helped the Zionist Movement in no small degree. See Chaim Weizmann, *Trial and Error*, pp. 191-92; Vera Weizmann, *The Impossible Takes Longer* (London: Hamish Hamilton, 1967), pp. 34, 90, 192-93. Mrs Weizmann reports that when her husband explained his theory for the production of high-octane aviation fuel from starches to the British Colonial Secretary Lord Lloyd, this exclaimed, 'Dr Weizmann, if you can do that, I shall become a Zionist!' (p. 193). The part played by Weizmann's contributions in the process that led to the issuance of the Balfour Declaration in 1917 is well known.

[6] Speech delivered on 2 November, 1949, at the dedication of the new Institute of Physics and Physical Chemistry at the Weizmann Institute, quoted in Meyer W. Weisgal and Joel Carmichael, eds. *Chaim Weizmann: A Biography by Several Hands* (London: Weidenfeld and Nicolson, 1962), p. 352.

nuclear programme had been laid, and a group of young scientists, brought together within the framework of the Ministry of Defence,[7] were sent abroad for specialization in different branches of advanced nuclear science. Five of these men—de Shalit, Yekutieli, Goldring, Talmi, and Pelah—returned in 1953 and 1954 after having studied in Holland, Switzerland, Britain and the United States and obtained practical experience in the latter country. Soon after, a Department of Nuclear Physics was set up in the Weizmann Institute at Rehovoth, where a Department of Isotope Research had been established as early as 1949. This earlier department had carried out intensive research in fields such as the exploitation of low-grade uranium ore, and the enrichment of heavy water by fractional distillation. As a result, a chemist, Professor Israel Dostrovsky, present Director-General of the Israeli Atomic Energy Commission, had developed a process for the production of heavy water which was not based on electric power and which he had earlier initiated at London University. This raised hopes of providing a competitive alternative to the heavy water produced in Norway through hydroelectric power and of breaking the Norwegian monopoly.[8]

At the same time, experiments were being carried out on the extraction of uranium from the phosphate ores of the Negev, resulting by the early 1950s in the development, on a pilot-plant scale, of a sufficiently economic process to warrant large-scale production.[9]

CREATION OF THE ATOMIC ENERGY COMMISSION

In mid-1952, the Ben-Gurion Government decided the time had come to create an organ which would co-ordinate and supervise all activities connected with atomic energy on a national scale. The need for such a central Authority, which would fulfil the tasks of long-range planning, was being particularly felt at a time when local production of uranium from phosphate ores was ready to advance beyond the laboratory stage, and a certain foreign Power —France—was evincing considerable interest in the Israeli 'chemical' method for heavy-water production.

The Israel Atomic Energy Commission (IAEC) was established

[7] See *ibid.*, Ch. 13, 'The Prisoner of Rehovoth,' by R. H. S. Crossman, pp. 342-50 for an account of how the scientific community in Jerusalem and Rehovoth was recruited by the military, its contributions to the war effort and Weizmann's critical attitude.
[8] *Bergmann Broadcast.*
[9] *Ibid.*; *Eytan Interview.*

on 13 June, 1952,[10] also within the framework of the Defence Ministry, and provided with an independent budget and laboratories of its own. It was headed by Dr Ernst David Bergmann—who was the Head of the Research and Planning Branch that had made the Negev uranium discovery and had been scientific director of the Weizmann Institute as well as one of Weizmann's closest collaborators—and consisted of five other members, viz., Dr Israel Dostrovsky, former Chief of Staff General Dori, Professor Cohen, Professor Racah, and Professor Samburski who was Chairman of the Scientific Council under the Prime Minister's Office.[11] The Commission was assigned the following tasks: (a) to advise the government on long-term policies and priorities in the advancement of nuclear research and development; (b) to supervise the implementation of officially approved policies; and (c) to represent Israel in her relations with scientific institutions abroad and international organizations engaged in nuclear research and development.[12]

Two things should be noted about the prerogatives granted to the AEC. First, it was assigned an advisory and supervisory role, and was not officially given decision-making powers in the field of nuclear energy. Secondly, within these limitations, there was no attempt sharply to define its range of action or even its *modus operandi*, at least in a final and codified manner, to the extent that the Commission was given no special statutes or by-laws. Only after its reorganization in 1966 was a Working Group on legislation formed.[13] This contrasts with the situation in France, for example, where the Commissariat à l'Energie Atomique was accorded 'multiple functions and substantial powers' whereby it 'directs, conducts or oversees not only scientific research projects but also the industrial development of atomic energy ...'[14] It may be explained as reflecting a desire to avoid the decentralization of decision-making in the nuclear field and limit such decision-making to the highest levels of political and military authority in the country. At the same time, by keeping the AEC's functions fluid, and its statutes unwritten, it would be possible to assign to it new tasks and prerogatives without having to go through the legislative

[10] *Bergmann Broadcast.*
[11] *Haboker* (Tel Aviv), 11 November, 1954.
[12] Israel Government, *Year Book: 1967/68* (Jerusalem: Government Printer, 1968), p. 57.
[13] United Nations, Educational, Scientific and Cultural Organization, *World Directory of National Science Policy-Making Bodies*, 1968, Vol. II, p. 67.
[14] Lawrence Scheinman, *Atomic Energy Policy in France Under the Fourth Republic* (Princeton, NJ: Princeton University Press, 1965), p. 8.

machinery, with the avoidance of unwanted publicity and public debate. This would save the tight secrecy which has consistently surrounded Israel's atomic establishment ever since its inception from impairment through legislative intervention. An example of the extremes to which this policy of secrecy was carried, even in the earliest stages of the programme, is the fact that the existence itself of the AEC was unknown to the Israeli public until its revelation by Chairman Bergmann in a special broadcast over Kol Yisrael on 19 November, 1954.[15]

As to why atomic research and its supervision were totally concentrated within the framework of the Defence Ministry, an official justification was provided by government circles in December 1960, during the crisis that followed the disclosure that Israel was building a large research reactor in the Negev. A government official alleged that, first, it had been the Ministry's Research and Planning Branch that had made the first uranium discoveries in 1948, and, second, when in 1955 Israel obtained American aid for the construction of the Nahal Soreq reactor, the Army had been thought to possess the technical know-how and organization to build it more cheaply and efficiently; so it had been decided to concentrate all nuclear enterprises in the Defence Ministry for reasons of administrative efficiency.[16] To this must be added other more complex and probably more compelling motives, stemming from the exalted status enjoyed by the military establishment in the political-institutional make-up, and its practically unlimited influence at a time when its main architect, David Ben-Gurion, was both Premier and Defence Minister (1948-1953 and 1955-1963). The fact that the country was practically in an open-ended state of war and the greater ability of the defence establishment to maintain secrecy must have also influenced Israeli calculations in this regard.

Once established, the AEC 'defined its two principal aims as follows: to discover possibilities of obtaining the radio-active minerals for industrial production of uranium and to work from the factors which Dr Dostrovsky's work in the Weizmann Institute had provided a process for the production of heavy water.'[17] Thus, a premium was laid on research aimed at the development of methods of production that would open new paths to the obtainment of two of the most basic and scarce raw materials in the field of nuclear power, namely, uranium and heavy water.

[15] *Bergmann Broadcast.*
[16] *The Times* (London), 20 December, 1960.
[17] *Bergmann Broadcast.*

In the late 1940s and early 1950s, the supply of these raw materials available on the world market was very limited. American policy was then already directed at preventing the diffusion of nuclear weapons (the United States and the Soviet Union being the only two countries to have atomic explosives at that time) and the United States and Britain had formed a Combined Development Agency with the purpose of purchasing all available uranium on the market, which was then shared between the two countries. As for heavy water, Norway, with its rich sources of hydroelectric power, was the only non-nuclear country producing this moderator on an industrial scale, and most of it was also ending up in the United States under an American-Norwegian agreement.[18] If alternative methods for the procurement of these materials could be discovered by Israeli scientists, the argument ran, this would provide Israel with trump cards which, if well played, would give the country's own nuclear programme a considerable push ahead in a short time. Such discoveries would represent very valuable assets which could then be traded off for the technological know-how, experience and installations that were necessary to carry out a serious nuclear reactor programme.

The French-Israeli deal of 1953 clearly suggests that these calculations were not off the mark.

ATOMIC CO-OPERATION WITH FRANCE

Though it was signed in the first half of 1953, the French-Israeli agreement on co-operation in the atomic field was not made public until November 1954, when Jules Moch, France's UN representative and former Defence Minister, disclosed in New York the existence of an agreement whereby France had purchased the patent of the Dostrovsky method for the production of heavy water.[19] This was further confirmed by the Israeli representative, Ambassador Abba Eban, who on 15 November declared before the Political and Security Committee of the General Assembly that a pilot plant for the production of heavy water was already operating in Israel and that the process 'has been adapted and applied in France.'[20] Simultaneously, in Tel Aviv, Prime Minister Moshe

---

[18] Scheinman, *op. cit.*, p. 23n. A moderator is a material used in a nuclear reactor to slow down neutrons from the high speeds at which they are produced in fission so as to enable the reaction to sustain itself.

[19] *Haboker*, 17 November, 1954; Michel Bar-Zohar, *Suez—Ultra Secret* (Paris: Fayard, 1964), p. 62.

[20] *Eban Speech.*

Sharett informed the Knesset that France and Israel had concluded an agreement for co-operation in atomic research.[21] Signed between the Israel AEC and the French CEA, the agreement provided for extensive exchange of information on atomic matters and for close co-operation between the nuclear scientists of the two countries. IAEC Chairman Bergmann revealed a few days later that 'young Israeli researchers have worked in the French laboratories and French researchers have worked and are working in Israeli installations.'[22]

French interest in Israeli atomic research was first evinced as early as 1949. In July of that year, one of the most important scientific figures in the French atomic programme, Professor Francis Perrin, visited Israel. The purposes of this visit were not revealed at the time, but it launched a close scientific co-operation in several fields, including the nuclear, between the two countries.[23] In April 1951, Francis Perrin was appointed High Commissioner of Atomic Energy and became the scientific Head of the French CEA. A few months later, the Commissariat reached a final decision on an important question that was to affect the whole future of the French nuclear programme, namely, whether to construct research reactors—which would be fuelled with enriched uranium that had to be imported—or undertake the production of fissionable material (plutonium) by high-power, natural uranium-fuelled reactors. For several reasons, among them the assurance of atomic independence that the second alternative would provide, the CEA decided to go into plutonium production.[24]

The importance of this decision from the point of view of French-Israeli atomic relations is that it made it imperative for France to develop or acquire methods to obtain natural uranium from the different grades of ore it possessed. The method developed by the Israelis for the processing of low-grade uranium ores such as phosphates had the double advantage of being also applicable to low-grade ores other than phosphates,[25] and of having been already tried and found workable and economically viable. Large quantities of heavy water would also be needed for the several reactors that were planned, and the Israelis had developed a cheaper method

[21] *Jerusalem Post*, 16 November, 1954; *Haboker*, 17 November, 1954.

[22] *Bergmann Broadcast*.

[23] Bar-Zohar, *op. cit.*, p. 49. See chapter III for more details on Israeli-French collaboration in the military and scientific fields.

[24] Scheinman, *op. cit.*, pp. 65-66.

[25] *Eytan Interview*.

than the electrolytic one utilized by Norway.

These two factors must have rendered an agreement with Israel highly attractive to the French. In effect, soon after the first French five-year plan for nuclear development—which embodied the decision to engage in plutonium production and provided for its implementation[26]—was adopted, the agreement between the French and Israeli atomic commissions was signed, early in 1953.[27]

France acquired the patent of the Israeli chemical process for heavy water production, which it proceeded to adapt industrially through the application of its own technological know-how. Also, important quantities of heavy water produced at the Weizmann Institute were shipped to France.[28] Though it was not mentioned at the time, France also acquired the right to use the low-grade uranium extraction process by this agreement; that this method came to be used by the French was admitted by them in December 1960.[29] In 1962, a leading figure in the French nuclear programme confirmed that the 1953 agreement had 'provided for technical exchanges with the Israeli Atomic Commission on heavy-water production and the processing of low-grade uranium ores'.[30]

In exchange, the Israelis gained access to a large part of French atomic knowledge and installations. Undoubtedly, they were also given an undertaking of French technical and material assistance in the construction of a reactor at a later date. Though no concrete evidence of such an undertaking has been made public, the sizable extent of the Israeli contribution under the terms of the agreement must obviously have been matched by a similarly considerable French contribution. The Israelis can hardly have given away their two main achievements in the field—in fact, all their atomic 'capital'—without assuring to themselves a commensurate return. Moreover, it should be remembered that in early 1953 announcement of the Eisenhower 'Atoms for Peace' programme, which made American reactor technology available to the world, was still many months in the future, that circulation of technical information therefore was extremely restricted or non-existent, and that the assistance of a power relatively advanced in the atomic research field, such as France, seemed absolutely essential at that early stage if Israel

[26] Scheinman, *op. cit.*, pp. 85-87.
[27] *Bergmann Broadcast.*
[28] *Le Monde* (Paris), 17 November, 1954.
[29] *Sunday Times* (London), 25 December, 1960.
[30] Bertrand Goldschmidt, *The Atomic Adventure: Its Political and Technical Aspects* (English Edition, London and New York: Pergamon & MacMillan, 1964), p. 83.

wished to acquire nuclear installations in the foreseeable future.

In short, French nuclear co-operation enabled Israel, first, to obtain a wealth of technical data and information; secondly, train its scientists and technicians at installations considerably more developed and sophisticated than its own; and, thirdly, profit from the experience of scientists who had a headstart of many years in the field. In other words, it provided Israel with the opportunity quickly to move ahead into a relatively large reactor programme at a much faster pace than most other small countries.

Though Professor Dostrovsky's process was extremely useful in attracting French interest, it does not seem to have proved economically viable for the Israelis themselves. The far more modest needs of their nuclear programme, both for research and for use in the Dimona reactor, have been filled through importation. In 1963, for example, the Technion Institute at Tel Aviv bought four tons of heavy water from the USAEC.[31] This shipment was naturally covered by American safeguards and was destined for research. It clearly indicates however that the increase in centres of deuterium production throughout the world since the mid-1950s, the consequent fall in prices and easier availability are all factors that have rendered the Israeli method uneconomical.

Dostrovsky's invention nonetheless has been successfully applied to the production of heavy oxygen isotopes (O^{18} and O^{17}) that are used as tracers in medicine, agriculture, biology and many other fields. Since 1949, when the heavy water plant at the Weizmann Institute in Rehovoth was constructed, Israel has grown into the world's main exporter of heavy oxygen.[32]

While France thus helped to lay the basic groundwork of the Israeli programme by opening her own atomic establishment to Israel's scientists and providing valuable information in the formative years,[33] it was the United States that gave the country its first

[31] New York Times, 27 October, 1963; USAEC Annual Report to Congress, 1965 (Washington, DC: Government Printing Office, 1966).

[32] The heavy water used in reactors is heavy in its hydrogen component (deuterium). The Weizmann Institute plant produces about 2500 grammes of O^{18} annually. The price of one gramme is around $500. See Joseph Wechsberg, A Walk through the Garden of Science: A Profile of the Weizmann Institute (London: Weidenfeld and Nicolson, 1967), chapter 19, for a non-technical description of the plant and the production process.

[33] It is interesting to note that, while both Israeli and French nuclear interests were furthered by the co-operation agreement, this also answered other, political and psychological, needs of the two countries. In 1952-54, Israel felt herself in an acute state of 'isolation' as a result of British approaches to the Arab states in an attempt to bring them together under the aegis of the Baghdad Pact, and of American pursuit of a 'northern tier'

reactor, under the terms of an agreement concluded in 1955, and assumed for the rest of the decade the role of prime supplier and mentor of its nuclear effort.

---

defence system against the Soviet Union. Britain was also negotiating the withdrawal of her 'buffer' forces from the Suez Canal area with the Egyptian revolutionary government, and even the Tripartite Declaration issued in 1950 was, as Israeli Premier Sharett put it, 'directed equally to Israel and the Arab States' (speech in the Knesset, *Jerusalem Post*, 15 November, 1954). For Israel, the agreement with France provided a sort of reinsurance, particularly in its military implications. For France, it was a means of returning to the area through a side-window, after both her Atlantic partners had eased her out of her traditional influential position in the Levant and ignored her in their on-going diplomatic offensives.

CHAPTER II

Nahal Soreq

ON 8 December, 1953, President Eisenhower announced in his famous 'Atoms for Peace' address at the UN General Assembly that the United States was willing to make some of her atomic knowledge and installations available to other countries for peaceful nuclear research. This was followed with the passage in the following August of the Atomic Energy Act of 1954, which permitted the exchange of hitherto restricted data and allowed the release of atomic materials for research and industrial use. As a result, about thirty bilateral agreements for nuclear co-operation between the United States and other countries, among which were Israel and Egypt, were signed over the next two years.[1]

The Agreement with Israel was entered into on 12 July, 1955, following contacts made early in the same year by the Israeli Ambassador in Washington, Abba Eban, with the chief American 'Atoms-for-Peace' negotiator, Morehead Patterson. It provided for a broad exchange of information on research reactors and their use and the transfer of up to six kilogrammes of 20 per cent enriched uranium^{235}.[2] At the same time, Israel was given the right to acquire an American-made small research reactor with the United States contributing $350,000 towards its cost. On 31 August, a technical library consisting of some 6,500 USAEC research and development reports, and about 45 bound volumes on nuclear theory and abstracts of reports and articles was presented to Israel.[3]

Between 1955 and 1960, some 56 Israelis were trained in American facilities, either on individual assignments or as participants in

[1] This and subsequent information on American nuclear policies and programmes abroad appearing in this chapter has been obtained from US Congress, Joint Committee on Atomic Energy, *Background Material for the Review of the International Atomic Policies and Programs of the United States*, by Robert McKinney, Joint Committee Print (Washington, DC: Government Printing Office, 1960), Vols. II and III. (Hereafter cited as *Background Report*.)
[2] Text in *United States Treaties and Other International Agreements*, Vol. 6, Part 2, 1955, pp. 2641-46.
[3] *New York Times*, 1 September, 1955.

USAEC-sponsored courses at the Oak Ridge Institute of Nuclear Studies and the International Institute of Nuclear Science and Engineering at the Argonne National Laboratory. Also, 24 Israeli scientists visited different USAEC installations.[4]

In many respects, the year 1955 was an eventful one for the promoters of Israel's nuclear programme. The First International Conference on the Peaceful Uses of Atomic Energy which was held in Geneva in August under United Nations sponsorship provided an opportunity for Israel to acquaint the scientific world with her progress in the atomic field. In its report to the Conference, the Israeli delegation—led by the Director-General of the Foreign Ministry Walter Eytan, with IAEC Chairman E. D. Bergmann as his deputy —disclosed that production of uranium as a by-product of the phosphates industry was under way. Throughout the year, several statements by top Israeli officials highlighted the country's advances in nuclear research. The then Defence Minister and Premier-designate, David Ben-Gurion, repeatedly expressed his belief that within a few years atomic power would have become the country's main source of energy, and that Israel could already build her own reactor with the locally-produced uranium and heavy water at her disposal.[5] This potential was also stressed by the Director-General of the Defence Ministry, Shimon Peres, a protegé of Ben-Gurion and one of the most active proponents of a military nuclear capability.[6]

In fact, this optimism was only partially due to the high expectations that were generally shared in those years regarding the promise of cheap atom-generated power, and which were widely advertised at the Geneva parley, particularly by the nuclear powers. The 'Atoms for Peace' Agreement with the Americans was also only one of the factors that augured well for Israel's nuclear future. The spate of statements and predictions that followed one another were primarily the expression of one facet of an important reorientation in Israel's defence posture that had followed the return to power of Ben-Gurion in February 1955.

The re-instatement of Ben-Gurion as Defence Minister on 17

---

[4] *Background Report*, II, p. 491.

[5] *New York Times*, 18 July; 27 September, 1955. A statement to the same effect was made by Eytan at the Geneva Conference, *Jerusalem Post*, 11 August, 1955.

[6] *Jerusalem Post*, 3 October, 1955. From an interview granted by Peres to the weekly *Jewish Observer and Middle East Review* in July 1965 it may be gleaned that the Defence Establishment had first proposed the building of the Dimona reactor in the course of 1955, *Jewish Observer*, (London), 9 July, 1965, pp. 14-15.

February came after the resignation of Pinhas Lavon as a result of a security 'mishap'[7] (the failure of an Israeli intelligence sabotage operation in Egypt) that added fuel to an already heated debate at the highest level on Israel's defence posture *vis-à-vis* the Arab countries. His take-over of the premiership in November after general elections in which Mapai, the ruling majority party, lost five seats signified the victory of the extremist 'hawkish' attitude on defence over the moderate policies of *rapprochement* advocated by Premier Sharett and the older leftist leaders of Mapai.[8] The Ben-Gurion faction, spearheaded by Peres and by the Army Chief-of-Staff Moshe Dayan, immediately set about strengthening the country's conventional military potential with the help of France, which was gradually realizing that Israel could be a very useful ally against Nasser, who had become enemy number-one through his assistance to the Algerian guerrillas. Simultaneously, increasing efforts were exerted to expand the nuclear establishment with a view to developing a weapons capability that would add to the Israeli deterrent.[9] This second task was to be pursued on two levels, one open and the other secret. Open activities included the association with the International Atomic Energy Agency (IAEA) after the Geneva Conference, the Agreement with the United States, and the construction of the Nahal Soreq Nuclear Centre, which was to house the 5-megawatt reactor, hot-laboratories for research and the Headquarters of the IAEC. Concurrently, but in utmost secrecy, the nuclear relationship with France was strengthened and, as we shall see, the accord for the construction of the Dimona plant was concluded soon after the joint adventure at Suez.

At the same time, a special division at the Defence Ministry was already engaged in rocketry research and another was promoting the development of an electronics industry.[10]

[7] For details of what became known as the Lavon 'affair' see Amos Perlmutter, 'The Israeli Army in Politics: The Persistence of the Civilian over the Military,' *World Politics*, Vol. 20, No. 4 (July 1968), pp. 630-36; Ben Halpern, 'The Military in Israel', in John Johnson, ed., *The Role of the Military in Under-Developed Countries* (Princeton, NJ: Princeton University Press, 1962), pp. 354-57; and Michael Bar-Zohar, *The Armed Prophet: A Biography of Ben-Gurion* (London: A. Barker, 1966), pp. 189-97.

[8] The struggle for power fought over Israel's defence policies and its consequences are authoritatively discussed in Amos Perlmutter, 'The Institutionalization of Civil-Military Relations in Israel: The Ben-Gurion Legacy and its Challengers,' *Middle East Journal*, Vol. 22, No. 4. Autumn 1968, pp. 415-32.

[9] *Ibid.*, pp. 421-22.

[10] *Jerusalem Post*, 3 October, 1955.

THE NUCLEAR ESTABLISHMENT

The keynote to the spirit in which the new Ben-Gurion government undertook these tasks was perhaps best sounded by the Prime Minister himself in a policy speech he delivered in the Knesset on November 2, the main theme of which appropriately was 'security':

> Security—that means the fostering of research and scientific achievement in all branches of physics, chemistry, geology, and technology and raising them to the highest standards. Scientific development is ... a necessary condition for the ... strengthening of our security....
>
> Today, science is the key to education, economic development, and military power.... Our security and independence require that more young people devote themselves to science and research, atomic and electronic research, research of solar energy ... and the like.[11]

These new developments in the area of defence policy and armaments were naturally unknown to the Israeli man in the street, who would not have probably lent them his support or seen them with approving eyes, particularly in regard to a nuclear capability. The mass extermination experiences of the 1940s—as well as Hiroshima and Nagasaki—were still fresh in the memories of the European Jews who in 1955 made up the largest proportion of the Israeli population, and the radical Socialist tradition was the most predominant streak in the political fabric of the society.[12] Geographical limitations were also acutely felt by all Israelis. At the same time, opinions were divided within the cabinet and the ruling Mapai party's leadership as to the suitability of developing an early nuclear capacity. For all these reasons, the Ben-Gurionites were restricted in their public advocacy of nuclear development to extolling the suitability of atomic energy as the source of supply for Israel's future power needs, and promoting the image of Israel as a country in an advanced technological and scientific stage that enabled it to construct reactors and benefit from the advantages provided by the harnessing of nuclear energy. The military factor was only indirectly introduced by the constant emphasis on the theme of scientific and technological progress as the key to Israel's future strength and the only guarantee of her long-term security.

Once again in full control of the country, and with a clearly

---

[11] Broadcast by the Israeli Home Service (Hebrew), 2 November, 1955.
[12] To this day, resistance to a military nuclear capability is strongest among the Socialists of the Mapam Party and leftist intellectuals.

formulated defence policy in process of implementation, Ben-Gurion lost no time and, a few months after his accession to the premiership, he entrusted a delegation of scientists with the task of selecting a research-reactor type for an Israeli facility. After visiting the United States, the group recommended a swimming-pool type and, on 19 March 1958, Israel signed a contract with the Atomics Division of the American Machine and Foundry Company of New York for the purchase of a 1-megawatt swimming-pool research reactor, the corresponding licence for which was issued by the USAEC on 12 June.[13] This model was chosen by the Israelis 'because of its simplicity and safe performance and because of the possibility of close approach to the reactor core under controlled conditions'.[14] Plans for the reactor building were made by Israeli engineers in co-operation with American scientists, and the ground was broken in November 1958 at Nahal Soreq, south of Tel Aviv, near the Weizmann Nuclear Research Centre in Rehovoth. Work was completed in May 1960, and the reactor became critical on 16 June of that year.[15]

Though originally of a 1,000-kilowatt rating, the Nahal Soreq reactor was designed to reach a capacity of 5,000 kilowatts (thermal). The estimated cost of the reactor was US $1,410,000,[16] and the approximate total cost of the complete installation amounted to three million dollars.[17] Fuelled with an enriched uranium-aluminium alloy provided by the United States under the 1955 Agreement, it uses natural water as both moderator and coolant. On 20 August, 1959, the Agreement was amended to provide for the increase in enrichment of the uranium from 20 per cent to 90 per cent, as this was deemed necessary for the efficiency of the reactor given its high neutron flux (10^{18}). The quantity of U-235 to be provided was also increased from six to ten kilogrammes. Comprehensive safeguard guarantees were included, as well as a statement of interest in the early transference of safeguards to the International Atomic Energy Agency. Under the Agreement, Israel obtains the enriched fuel on lease, pays 4 per cent of its value, returns it after

[13] US Atomic Energy Commission, *Annual Report to Congress, 1959* (Washington, DC: Government Printing Office, 1960), p. 472.
[14] Israel Atomic Energy Commission, *Israel Research Reactor IRR-1*, a Report compiled by R. S. Kahan (Rehovoth: IAEC, 1961), Introduction.
[15] Israel Government, *Year Book, 1960-61*, pp. 72-73.
[16] USAEC *Annual Report to Congress 1961*, p. 494.
[17] Leonard Beaton and John Maddox, *The Spread of Nuclear Weapons* (London: Chatto and Windus, 1962), p. 170.

burn-up and pays for the reduction in isotope content.[18]

Code-named 'IRR-1', the reactor was built by the Israeli Ministry of Defence for the IAEC.[19] Six kilogrammes of fuel are ensconced at the bottom of a 25 feet-deep pool filled with filtered natural water and surrounded by a concrete wall 8-feet thick at the base. The pile is controlled by a series of rods coated with cadmium and boron which regulate the flow of neutrons.[20]

Under the Atomic Energy Act of 1954, American co-operation in nuclear matters with other countries is subjected to 'a guaranty by the co-operating party that any material to be transferred pursuant to such agreement will not be used for atomic weapons or for research on or development of atomic weapons, or for any other military purposes'. As a result, a system of inspection visits was instituted to enforce this clause. The Nahal Soreq reactor was visited twice a year by American inspectors until 1965. These inspections included the verification of material inventories, the identification of items such as fuel elements and the observation of the reactor in operation to verify that at least a critical mass of fuel was present.[21]

In 1964, when the US-Israeli Agreement was up for renewal, the United States decided to transfer her safeguards functions to the IAEA, thus putting into effect the expression of intent included in the 1960 amendment. This decision was in line with the American policy of strengthening the safeguards system of the IAEA by having all countries in the 'Atoms for Peace' programme submit to it. Israel's relations with the IAEA have always been rather strained, as Israel holds that the regional representation system followed by the Agency in the appointment of its ruling body discriminates against her. Objections to the American decision led to extended negotiations in Washington,[22] which finally ended with the Israelis agreeing to IAEA safeguards and the new amended Agreement was signed on 2 April, 1965. Article VI bis, par. 8, of the Agreement as amended actually staked the future of continued American assistance to the Israeli nuclear effort on the transfer to the IAEA of the

---

[18] *Ibid.*, p. 171.
[19] *New York Times*, 5 July, 1960.
[20] Israel Pelah, 'The Israeli Atomic Research Reactor and its Uses,' *Madda* (Tel Aviv), February 1961, [in Hebrew].
[21] *Background Report*, III, 853.
[22] *New York Times*, 19 April, 1964. See also Peres, *David's Sling*, pp. 105-6.

safeguards function.[23] Israeli acceptance was important for the United States as the case was considered to be a test of American resolve to strengthen the international inspection system of the IAEA, and the price Washington paid for this acceptance became evident one year later when a further agreement between the two countries was signed amending and broadening the previous accord by the provision of 40 kilogrammes of enriched uranium.[24] Moreover, American agreement to consider joint construction of a large nuclear desalination plant in Israel seems to have further mollified the Israelis who then saw 'there was no point in maintaining our stubborness over the small reactor'.[25]

It is interesting to note that no inspection of the reactor by IAEA inspectors has reportedly taken place since the safeguard functions were transferred to this Organization by a trilateral Agreement signed between the United States, Israel and the IAEA on 18 June, 1965, and which entered into force on 15 June, 1966.[26] According to IAEA officials, this is standard procedure where small facilities of a rating not higher than 3 megawatts—which is not the Israeli case—are involved. This would imply that IAEA control of the Nahal Soreq reactor is now limited to the receipt of routine periodic reports on the movement of source and fissionable materials in and out of the facility and on the activities of the reactor. A degree of control is indirectly exercised by the donor country as well, since the spent fuel is shipped back to the United States for reprocessing, and all leased materials would thus have to be accounted for.

From a military point of view, then, the Nahal Soreq plant is of value as a training ground for scientist and technicians, and for nuclear research and development. Since plutonium is produced from uranium[238], the near absence of this isotope from the fuel of this reactor means that practically no fissile material is being produced. Though the highly-enriched uranium provided as fuel could be conceivably used as the explosive core for 3-4 nuclear warheads of the Hiroshima type, this would not only entail a unilateral termination of the Agreement by Israel and the illegal appropriation

[23] Text in *United States Treaties and Other International Agreements*, Vol. 16, Part 2, 1965, pp. 1773-74.
[24] Text in *United States Treaties and Other International Agreements*, Vol. 17, Part I, 1966, pp. 1365-67.
[25] Peres, *David's Sling*, p. 106.
[26] *Washington Post*, 13 March, 1969. For the text of the Agreement, see *United Nations Treaty Series*, Vol. 573R, No. 8320.

of the special material—an unlikely step for a country substantially dependent on United States good will—but would also probably require further enrichment of the U^{235} to attain the necessary weapons-grade purity, and none of the existing enrichment plants would be likely to accommodate the Israelis.[27] Future perfectioning of the gas-centrifuge enrichment process, in which Israeli scientists have reportedly evinced much interest, could eventually provide a local alternative. Nonetheless, the Dimona facility would suggest that an Israeli warheads programme would be based on plutonium-core weapons.

[27] Uranium enrichment plants exist at present in the United States, the Soviet Union, Britain, France, and China.

CHAPTER III

Dimona

THOUGH in any discussion of the military potentialities of the Israeli nuclear establishment the research reactor at Dimona in the northern Negev must loom much larger than the installations at Nahal Soreq, no comparable analysis of its characteristics and uses can unfortunately be made on account of the complete secrecy maintained in everything even remotely connected with this facility. A measure of the security precautions adopted by the government is given by the fact that to this date, the site is out-of-bounds even for Knesset members.[1] Discussion of the nuclear programme in the press is not tolerated.

The role played by this policy of blanket security will be discussed later on, but there is no doubt that its most immediate and obvious consequence is to make a large part of what is said about the present status of the nuclear programme verge on the speculative; there is no room for doubts, however, in so far as the impact of the reactor in a military sense is concerned.

Dimona was a by-product of Suez. The crisis of 1956, and particularly the decisive American stand, convinced France that, to be able to exercise the prerogatives of a world power and have a truly independent foreign policy, an atomic arsenal was necessary.[2] It also led to very close co-operation between that country and Israel, cemented by the joint military adventure in Egypt and later by the frustration they shared as to its outcome. The agreement to set up the reactor was reached in 1957, and its exact terms covering fuel supplies and other important details have remained secret to this day.

The resignation in 1957 of all the members of the Israel Atomic Energy Commission, with the exception of its Chairman, Professor Bergmann, seems to have been sparked off by the decision to build

---

[1] Aubrey Hodes, 'Implications of Israel's Nuclear Capability,' *The Wiener Library Bulletin* (London), XXII (Autumn, 1968), p. 3. See also p. 39.
[2] See Scheinman, *op. cit.*, pp. 171-3; C. L. Sulzberger, *The Test: De Gaulle and Algeria*, p. 25, cited in Yoram Nimrod, 'L'eau, l'atome et le conflit,' *Les Temps Modernes* (Paris), XXII, No. 253Bis, 1967.

this reactor on the part of the Ministry of Defence. This decision was strongly opposed by the scientists on grounds which, though still obscure, suggest that military uses figured rather prominently in the calculations of the decision-makers. Thus, in a lecture delivered at Tel Aviv, Professor Bergmann revealed that 'with two or three exceptions, the leaders of the country opposed this policy which they considered as *irresponsible*', adding that, 'despite technical and financial difficulties, the project was executed thanks to Ben-Gurion's visionary genius'.[3] In 1965, after leaving the post of Director-General of the Defence Ministry, Shimon Peres, a man who was closely associated with the Dimona project from the start (having been one of the architects of the French-Israeli military relationship), stated that many had at first criticized the project as 'an act of political adventurism that would unite the world against us,'[4] and a prominent member of Mapai spoke of it as 'a political, economic and military catastrophe.'[5] A strictly peaceful programme would have hardly elicited such reactions.

This on the internal level. Abroad, the disclosure by American intelligence in December 1960 that what Washington had been led to believe was a textile plant was actually a large and tightly guarded nuclear facility caused a major crisis in American-Israeli relations. The discovery was considered serious enough to warrant a closed-door unannounced meeting of the Joint Congressional Committee on Atomic Energy, held on 9 December and attended by State Department and Central Intelligence Agency officials. As a result, the United States formally asked Israel whether she was planning to go into nuclear weapons production. By 19 December, no answer had yet been received, and President Eisenhower was briefed on the importance attached by the Administration to the Israeli facility.[6] That same day, the French Foreign Ministry and the Israeli Embassy in Paris issued statements that confirmed the reports and avowed the existence of a joint endeavour to build a natural uranium-fuelled reactor in Israel. The French spokesman said the facility was similar to that supplied by Canada to India[7] and gave assurances that precautions had been taken to limit the

---

[3] Nimrod, *ibid.*, pp. 902-03. Emphasis added.
[4] *Jewish Observer and Middle East Review* (London), 9 July, 1965, pp. 14-15.
[5] Nimrod, *op. cit.*, p. 903.
[6] *New York Times*, 20 December, 1960.
[7] *Le Monde* (Paris), 20 December, 1960.

reactor's work to peaceful purposes.[8] This allegation has since been rejected by the Israelis. On 20 December, Prime Minister Ben-Gurion and Foreign Minister Golda Meir held top level consultations with senior government officials to 'formulate the government's official statement of policy on the Dimona reactor issue.'[9] Finally, on 21 December while Ambassador Harman delivered official assurances to Washington that his country was not engaged in nuclear weapons production, Ben-Gurion acknowledged in the Knesset that a 24,000 kilowatt (thermal) reactor was being constructed in the Negev with French assistance, stating that it would be devoted to peaceful uses. Scheduled for completion in 1964, it would be fuelled with natural uranium and moderated and cooled by heavy water. Of the 1957 agreement with France, not a single detail was released by either country.

The cost of the plant was estimated by Israeli sources in 1960 to be around 250 million Israeli pounds ($130 million).[10] The reliability of this estimate cannot be accurately assessed, however, as no figures have been released by the government. Indeed, in a report published in July 1961, the State Controller complained that clear estimates of the reactor's costs had been withheld even from the Knesset.[11]

The size of the natural uranium pile has not been revealed. Some experts consider it to be around 24 metric tons.[12] The Israeli Government has emphasized that the reactor itself is not subject to any French controls;[13] and, consequently, the only obstacle to Israeli self-sufficiency and independence from any outside interference as regards the nature of the reactor's work would be the problem of obtaining the natural uranium and heavy water requirements free of safeguards. The uranium problem will be further discussed in detail. The heavy water method developed by Dostrovsky apparently has not proved as economical as was originally expected.[14] The research base has been constantly expanding, however, and the provision of this particular material may have ceased to be a significant

---

[8] The Canada-India research reactor (CIR), with a rating of 40 Megawatts (thermal), was built in Bombay under the Colombo Plan and is not subject to safeguards. It became operational in 1960.

[9] *Jerusalem Post*, 21 December, 1960.

[10] *Ibid.*, 22 December, 1960.

[11] *New York Times*, 1 August, 1961.

[12] Leonard Beaton, *Must the Bomb Spread?* (Harmondsworth: Penguin Books in association with The Institute for Strategic Studies, 1966), p. 78.

[13] Beaton and Maddox, *op. cit.*, p. 172.

[14] *Ibid.*, p. 173. See also p. 23 above.

problem, particularly since the centres of production abroad have multiplied in recent years. Moreover, if it becomes necessary to obtain control-free heavy water for a weapons programme and no foreign sources prove available, local production by the Dostrovsky method may be resorted to in spite of the higher costs involved.

Activated in late 1964, the Dimona reactor has been unofficially 'visited' by American scientists, an arrangement instituted at the insistence of the Kennedy Administration so as to check on the nature of the work being done there. Visits were made by prominent American nuclear scientists in the spring of 1961 and in the summer of 1962 while the Dimona complex was being erected, and they reported that no chemical separation plant was under construction.[15] With the new Eshkol Government in power in 1964, this policy was continued and further 'inspections' were conducted in the spring of 1964, in February 1965, in June 1966 and shortly before the six-day war of 1967.[16] The visitors concluded that the reactor was being used for peaceful purposes, though this conclusion was avowedly *tentative*, as once-a-year inspections are insufficient to determine with certainty that no fuel rods are being removed for the purpose of extracting the plutonium produced during the operation of the pile[17], which would be sufficient to manufacture one Nagasaki-type bomb per year.

Furthermore, the visitors had charged that no adequate inspection was possible because of the 'hurried and limited nature' of the visits allowed. A team that visited the facility in 1969 reportedly submitted a written complaint, stating that 'it could not guarantee that there was no weapons-related work at Dimona' in view of the limitations imposed by the Israelis on its inspection procedures.[18]

Even this limited, informal and practically ineffective amount of supervision over the nature of Dimona's work was strongly resented by the Israelis. The Ben-Gurion Government only agreed to the institution of the American 'inspectorate' as a compromise arrangement after Washington's repeated requests that all nuclear facilities be submitted to international safeguards were refused, at the risk

[15] Hodes, *op. cit.*, p. 4.
[16] *New York Times*, 14 March, 1965; 28 June, 1966; 6 July, 1967.
[17] *Ibid.*, 28 June, 1966. When weapons-grade plutonium[239] is sought, the fissile material must be withdrawn from the reactor at fairly short intervals to avoid its contamination by Pu^{240}, which would render it militarily worthless in some cases. See pp. 75-76, 88 below.
[18] Hedrick Smith, 'US Assumes the Israelis Have A-Bomb or Its Parts,' *New York Times*, 18 July, 1970.

of a cut-off in American assistance in the atomic field.[19]

For the activist right-wingers who fathered and nursed the nuclear programme in the 1950s the yearly inspection visits meant not only an unwelcome interference with Israel's internal affairs in a vital security area, but a direct threat to the policy of 'keeping the Arabs guessing' as well. This strategy of 'deterrence through uncertainty',[20] which provides one of the major justifications for the blanket secrecy imposed on all nuclear activities, would be rendered ineffective in the opinion of its advocates by American assurances leaked to Israel's enemies that the Negev reactor is engaged in purely peaceful research. That the UAR has not yet found it necessary actively to seek the development of a nuclear capability or, at least, to mount a serious campaign for outside guarantees, contenting herself with a small Russian-built and serviced 2-megawatts reactor, may in itself be proof that assurances are being conveyed to Cairo by a United States concerned with avoiding a nuclear race in the area.

If such were the case, could it not be argued that if assurances are being actually given to the Arab governments, then the aims of the 'deterrence through uncertainty' approach are well served by the American inspections, since these would help in convincing the Arabs that there is really no immediate cause for alarm, thus preserving the considerable time-lead Israel has in nuclear development over her opponents? The answer to this would be two-fold.

Firstly, by promoting an image of scientific sophistication in the military (conventional *and* nuclear) sphere, the Israelis hope to deter their neighbours from overstepping certain limits—particularly during 'hot' wars but also during the 'semi-hot' intervals—such as mounting attacks against Israeli population centres, for example. The possibility of bombing raids against urban concentrations has always been seriously considered and feared by Israeli planners, particularly before the six-day war. The implication in this case would be that such qualitative escalation from battlefield warfare to mass bombardment of civilian targets might lead to an actuali-

[19] According to a reputedly well-informed source, the newly-installed Kennedy Administration did not stop short of 'pressure, sharply-worded Notes and veiled threats, [and] allusions to measures that the United States might employ,' in its desire to ascertain at first hand the true nature of the reactor's work, see Bar-Zohar, *The Armed Prophet*, p. 283.

[20] In this case, deterrence not of an enemy attack, but rather of the development of an opposite nuclear capability by the enemy by fostering in him the belief that it does not rate high enough on his scale of priorities. See chapter XI.

zation of the Israeli nuclear capability. For this implication to have credibility, the existence, or at least the belief by the enemy in the existence, of a nuclear threshold capability would be essential. It is this credibility that would be undermined by periodical American assurances.

Alternatively—or, rather, simultaneously—opposition to American inspection visits could be based on the apprehension that the visitors might eventually get wind of the existence of potentially non-peaceful activities at the Dimona facility, such as the production of weapons-grade plutonium. Though the chances of such a discovery being made would be undoubtedly small, since the visits have always taken place on dates set by the Israeli Government, a mere suspicion voiced by a scientist-guest or an unguarded statement could break the delicate psychological balance the Israelis apparently seek to maintain.

An interesting and illuminating exchange took place in the Knesset on 5 July, 1966, in the wake of a report in the *New York Times*[21] on that year's American visit to Dimona, that is worth quoting at some length:

YOHANAN BEDER (Gahal): ... What has been published by the *New York Times* is extremely serious, because we cannot know what [the inspectors] are saying, what they are leaking to Nasser's Ambassador, and other ambassadors. What guarantee do we have that when they leak such information to the *New York Times*— and all the world knows that they are leaking it—they are not also giving many more details to our enemies? I believe that the results of the research being carried on should not be made public. There is no country within my knowledge that undertakes research of this nature and publishes all its results. I presume that if the United States government, for example, were to deliver to France all its secrets and all its achievements in this field, France would not have to undertake research, because she would be getting everything on a silver platter. Should we invest in research to have the American experts deliver its results to our enemies?

In addition to all these essentially practical considerations, there is a more important matter ... Israel's honour and sovreignty.... What is the significance of having experts representing the United States government make periodic visits to the Dimona atomic research reactor? What does this mean? Are we

[21] 28 June, 1966.

introducing supervision to places that are closed even to Israel's citizens and even to the members of the Knesset themselves? What type of arrangements governs these visits? ... It has been said that they will take place annually. If this is so, then they cease to be courtesy visits, and our government will not succeed in convincing me that [the visitors] are coming out of courtesy, or that their visits are permitted as a gesture of good will, because we know from the *New York Times* that these visits are being set from one year to the next ...

LEVI ESHKOL (Prime Minister and Minister of Defence): ... I wish to say that in all its official activities Israel has fully protected its sovereignty. There has been neither control nor supervision—and I advise you to distinguish between a visit, control and supervision—on the part of any country over the Dimona atomic research reactor ...

* * *

Some visits have been made since 1961 by American scientists who were guests of the Israel government. This means on the basis of an invitation by the Israel government. An invitation is necessary from time to time. It would be impossible for them to come without an invitation.

I can assure the Knesset that we shall know how to protect ... Israel's sovereignty in all our affairs and in all matters related to security. It seems to me that there is no point in fearing the disclosure of secrets that are untrue. We should not fear or suspect that these guests, who come here as visitors, will tell anyone things that are untrue—and you have heard what they have said ...

I believe the Knesset will agree with me that no debate should be started here ... I therefore move that the debate be transferred to the Foreign Affairs and Security Committee and that no further discussion take place in the House plenum on what is, in any case, a very sensitive matter. [The motion was submitted to a vote and carried.]

* * *

MEIR VILNER (New Communist List): ... We are against this foreign supervision, and we are also against every thought and every action in the direction of nuclear armaments. We support denuclearization for our region. We believe that nuclear weapons are a deadly poison for Israel, and consequently renew from this forum our demand that the State of Israel, its Knesset, and its government agree to the denuclearization of our region, and that there be no atomic weapons, and that there be no preparation of atomic weapons, and that neither Israel nor the Arab countries seek these weapons from outside.

The government's position on the question of general regional disarmament in evading and even opposing international initiatives for regional nuclear disarmament under UN supervision adds a particular and menacing meaning to the Prime Minister's words 'sensitive matters' ...

SHIMON PERES (Rafi): ... the government, which has requested the transfer of the debate to the Foreign Affairs and Security Committee, is itself the main source of almost daily leaks to the press ... A government spokesman announced last week that these visits took place with the approval of the French. Why did he announce that? He declared that the visits do not affect the work there. Why did he declare that?

*   *   *

Members of the Knesset: I have just returned from a meeting where much was said on this subject ... I found that there is unfortunately no possibility of limiting the spread of nuclear weapons in the near future—not because of Israel, but because big powers are not agreeing among themselves ...

I was glad to discover that most experts on the subject do not believe it possible to envisage nuclear disarmament for the Middle East in isolation from the conventional arms race ...[22]

I see no reason why the State of Israel should reassure Nasser from this rostrum and let him know what we do and what we don't do. I know that the Arabs suspect [our nuclear intentions] and I know that this suspicion is a deterrent force. Then, why

[22] The meeting alluded to was the International Assembly on Nuclear Weapons, held on 23-26 June, 1966, in Toronto, Canada, and sponsored by the Institute for Strategic Studies, the American Assembly of Columbia University and other research institutions. Contrary to what Peres implied in this statement, the Assembly called for 'a serious effort' to 'negotiate a Nuclear Free Zone' for the Middle East. *Report of the International Assembly on Nuclear Weapons, 23-26 June, 1966*, Toronto, Canada, p. 8.

should we allay these suspicions, why should we elucidate them?...[23]

The actual military potential of the Dimona reactor, which has been characterized as 'particularly well-suited for producing the fissionable plutonium used in nuclear bombs,'[24] will be assessed in Part II. In general terms, it can be said to represent an obvious, deliberate attempt by Israel to acquire a military nuclear option by developing an *independent* nuclear capability which, though comparatively small, could have far-reaching, perhaps decisive, effects in any political as well as military regional confrontation.

[23] Israel Government, *Records of the Knesset* (Divrei Haknesset), Sixth Knesset, First Session, Vol. 28, 5 July, 1966, pp. 2023-27. [Unofficial translation from Hebrew.]

[24] *New York Times*, 20 December, 1960. The Israeli reactor has been reported as being of the same type as the large American facility at Savannah, SC, which has provided the United States with a sizable part of its plutonium stockpile.

CHAPTER IV

Nuclear Infrastructure and Policy-making Bodies

THOUGH interest primarily focuses on reactors whenever a country's nuclear effort is discussed, an accurate assessment of its actual significance in military terms is not possible without due consideration of the complex scientific and industrial back-up structure that is essential to convert the fissionable material created in the heart of a reactor into a finished weapon ready for deployment and utilization by the armed forces. That this support set-up is an absolute requirement where modern weapons systems are concerned is certainly realized by the men directly in charge of Israel's security, and they have consistently sought to enlist the country's scientists in defence-oriented work, as well as actively encouraged the development of science-based industries since, 'the development of modern means of warfare ... depends on a nation having a modern, bold and highly developed science, industry and technology.'[1]

This chapter will attempt, first, briefly to assess the Israeli nuclear programme's infrastructure in terms of important ancillary installations and its technological and scientific manpower potential; and, secondly, to examine the different sources of policy that have a role to play in determining the shape, orientation and goals of the programme. Though details on instruments, installations and processes are included, the stress is primarily laid on the human element, both from the standpoint of scientific know-how and specialized skills essential to master the difficult operations involved in reactor technology as well as atomic weapons production, and in regards to the actual shaping of policy in the field. The role of the military in policy-making is given particular attention.

PLANT AND RESEARCH FACILITIES

The two basic components of any nuclear effort are, in addition to manpower requirements, the specialized installations that together form what has been called the nuclear fuel cycle, and the facilities

---

[1] Shimon Peres, 'Israel's Defence in the Modern Age,' *Israel Year Book 1965* (Tel Aviv: no date), p. 32.

reserved for research and development. The tendency of the Israel Atomic Energy Commission apparently has been to concentrate fundamental, or pure, research in the principal institutions of higher learning, while entrusting defence-oriented applied research to the Ministry of Defence's considerable scientific staff and to the Negev Nuclear Centre at Dimona.

As far as the actual plant is concerned, the present status of the Israeli nuclear fuel cycle is discussed later on in connection with fuel procurement.[2] It is evident however that, in addition to the reactors at Nahal Soreq and Dimona, the IAEC has several other subsidiary installations of vital importance for their potential as key components of a weapons production process. Foremost among these are the 'hot laboratories' that were built with British assistance near Nahal Soreq for the processing of radioactive matter produced by the reactor. These laboratories are equipped—through American aid—with special remote control and automatic instruments necessary to handle highly toxic material. Similar facilities have been constructed as part of the Dimona complex to deal with the irradiated elements produced by the reactor there.

The military significance of these installations lies primarily in the experience and training they provide in the difficult art of handling irradiated material. Such skills would be extremely useful for the eventual construction and operation of the chemical separation plant that would have to be set up in order to obtain the plutonium produced at Dimona in the purified form necessary for the manufacture of the bomb cores. A measure of the sophistication of the laboratory facilities at the Negev Centre is given by the quality of research being conducted there, as shown by published unclassified papers.[3]

As for the Soreq Research Centre, the fact of its being an open facility and its proximity to the Weizmann Institute of Science (at Rehovoth some seven miles away) have turned it into a principal nucleus of pure and applied research into the peaceful uses of atomic energy. The Centre has adequate facilities and has undergone considerable expansion in the last ten years, both in staff and output.[4] Between 1961 and 1966, the Centre's staff increased from 74 to 188, and there was an eleven-fold increase in rate of publication. Its

[2] See Chapter VI.
[3] See Antoine Zahlan, *Science and Higher Education in Israel* (Beirut: The Institute for Palestine Studies, 1970), for an evaluation in depth of Israeli scientific research.
[4] Zahlan, *op. cit.*, pp. 106-07.

importance for the Israeli nuclear effort lies in part in its being the one venue for contact with the international scientific community that is operated and controlled by Israelis, since the Dimona facility is completely 'off-limits' in this respect. In other words, it is at Nahal Soreq that Israel receives its scientist guests and exchange researchers, and profits from the interaction of local and foreign know-how and experience that is essential in the complex and ever-expanding nuclear field. It is significant that the great majority of the scientific reports and research papers submitted by Israelis at international nuclear conferences and symposia are based on work done at Nahal Soreq. While this is naturally explained by the need to preserve Dimona's secrecy, it enhances the importance of Nahal Soreq as Israel's 'passport' to world nuclear science.

Other advanced research and development facilities are those at the Institute of Nuclear Science in the Weizmann Institute of Science, at Rehovoth. The principal piece of equipment there is a 15 Mev Van de Graaff proton accelerator used in the study of nuclear reactions and properties through the bombardment of atoms with neutrons or protons. This Tandem atom-smasher was acquired with funds provided by the West German government and is run jointly with the Hebrew University. It started operating in 1965 when it replaced a 3 Mev accelerator, installed in 1958.[5] The Nuclear Institute's buildings contain some 71 laboratories, as well as electronic and mechanical workshops. The Weizmann Institute actually has been the scientific nerve-centre of the whole nuclear programme. The Applied Mathematics Department has developed and put together advanced computers.[6] The Dostrovsky heavy water production method was developed there, and the Department of Nuclear Physics has undertaken research for several foreign bodies under contract, including the US Air Force and Navy, as well as Euratom. The Institute's scientists have also done secret work for the USAEC.[7]

The Israel Institute of Technology, also known as the Technion, in Haifa is another important contributor to the nuclear effort. This Institute established in 1958 a special Department of Nuclear Science

[5] The Weizmann Institute of Science, *Scientific Activities 1967* (Rehovoth, 1968), p. 269.
[6] There were 81 computers in Israel at the end of 1967, five of which were manufactured locally. This figure had gone up to 158 at the end of 1969 and reached 172 by May 1970.
[7] *New York Times*, 19 December, 1960; Israel Government, *Year Book: 1965/66*, pp. 83-84.

and Engineering for the express purpose of training scientists in reactor technology and of providing technical personnel for the two reactors then under construction.[8] Also, fuel element studies were carried out there by Dr Shimon Yiftah, who has worked at the Argonne National Laboratory in the United States, and is the author of a standard work on fast reactors.

Several people connected with fuel elements work were sent abroad for further study and came back in 1962-63.[9] This clearly indicates a determination to achieve self-sufficiency in the furnishing of natural uranium fuel elements for the Dimona reactor and other future piles. A fuel element factory is necessary to prepare the uranium metal obtained locally or imported from abroad for utilization in the reactor. Fuel preparation and processing is a long operation, involving a number of complex steps. Typical operations are the chemical conversion of the uranium compound to the metallic or oxide form, vacuum casting of metals, and machining, rolling, extruding, drawing, pelletizing, grinding or swaging the fuel elements into the form or dimensions required by the reactor. The burn-up efficiency of the reactor, and consequently its economical use, depends to a large extent on the proper preparation of the fuel elements. The use of the uranium produced from Negev phosphates implies that a fuel elements plant forms part of the Dimona complex.

Finally, the scientific research force of the Ministry of Defence and the Ministry's well-equipped laboratories provide a further addition of capital importance to the over-all nuclear effort. Defence-connected research and development has always been under the aegis and exclusive control of this department and, though no official figures are available as to the extent of the facilities and budget allotted thereto, an approximate idea of the considerable set-up involved is given by such indicators as the development of a rocket programme that yielded encouraging results as early as 1961,[10] a nuclear instrumentation and servicing industry and a rapidly advancing aerospace technology that has recently produced its first

[8] Gerald Tauber, *Scientific Endeavor of Israel* (New York: Herzl Press, 1961), p. 14.
[9] Beaton and Maddox, *op. cit.*, p. 174.
[10] See Chapter VIII. Israel has locally developed a surface-to-surface naval tactical missile called *Gabriel* which became operational in early 1970. It reportedly has a maximum range of 13 miles, carries a 330-lb warhead, and speeds to its target at 280 miles per hour sixty feet above the water level. *Revue de défense nationale* (Paris), January 1970, p. 167.

locally-manufactured aircraft.[11]

Israel is a country uniquely endowed in her scientific and technological manpower resources and has therefore been spared what is
perhaps the most serious obstacle faced by any country desirous of
mounting a nuclear programme, namely, the training and assembling of a large force of physicists, chemists, engineers, technicians,
managers and skilled workers capable of setting up and maintaining one of the most difficult, complex and advanced technologies in
existence. The flow of Western Jews into Palestine, from the prominent German professors who were driven out in the 1930s by the
Nazi menace and recruited by Weizmann for the Daniel Sieff Institute at Rehovoth,[12] to the thousand scientists and engineers who
formed part of the first wave of immigrants after the creation of the
state in 1948,[13] and the many more who gradually followed them
to reside permanently in Israel, has resulted in a remarkable concentration of high-level manpower that is constantly added to by
the graduate output of, particularly, the Hebrew University, the
Haifa Technion, and the Weizmann Institute. Most of these gradu-
ates, moreover, are in the natural sciences and, as will be seen, this
is the result of a systematic policy fostered by the defence establishment. An index of this bias in Israeli higher education, which is
particularly acute at the post-graduate level, is that not more than
ten per cent of all PhD candidates are working for a degree in the
humanities, law or the social sciences.[14] In 1967-68, graduate and
undergraduate students in sciences and engineering at the three
previously mentioned institutions totalled 7,500, of whom 437 were
doctoral candidates.[15] In 1963, fourteen out of every thousand working persons in Israel were holders of academic degrees in science
or engineering.[16]

[11] The STOL (short take-off and landing) passenger and transport light
aircraft 'Arava', which had its first test flight on 27 November, 1969,
International Herald Tribune, 28 November, 1969. The Israel Aircraft
Industries also produce the Fouga Magister jet trainer under French licence
and the recently acquired Jet Commander.
[12] The Sieff Institute was opened on 3 April, 1934 by the Sieff, Marks
and Sacher families of England at Weizmann's prompting, and was later
on enlarged and reorganized as the Weizmann Institute of Science, in 1949.
[13] Shaul Katz, *Science in Israel 1968* (Jerusalem: Publications Service of
the Prime Minister's Office, 1968), p. 2.
[14] Zahlan, *op. cit.*, p. 39.
[15] *Ibid.*, p. 37.
[16] Katz, *op. cit.*, p. 2. See Zahlan, *op. cit.*, chapter II for a detailed analysis
of the Israeli labour force, particularly its high-level manpower component.

NUCLEAR INFRASTRUCTURE

Though no figures are obtainable regarding the total number of scientists and engineers currently engaged in work connected with the nuclear effort, both operational and research, an estimate of 1,500 would err on the conservative side. The Atomic Energy Commission alone employs 300 scientists and has a technical staff of 600.[17] Other laboratories under the Ministry of Defence engage a large scientific personnel whose work on weapons research, electronics and other defence-connected areas is essential for the development of a military nuclear capability.[18]

This all goes to prove that the scientific know-how and skilled manpower requirements of a nuclear weapons programme, as well as the basic research substructure and the major part of the nuclear fuel cycle, are available to a large extent at present. An intensification of efforts would certainly be called for if a weapons programme is launched, but no major difficulties should be expected from this quarter in a country which is characterized by an unusually high concentration of scientific and technological expertise relative to population. If about 100 professional scientists and engineers are considered sufficient to run a small plutonium production programme,[19] Israel's current potential is several times this figure, and the country already possesses considerable ancillary equipment and installations. Moreover, the manpower requirements of a modest programme designed to produce nuclear weapons on a continuous basis, recently estimated as approximately 1,300 engineers and 500 scientists,[20] are clearly well within present Israeli capabilities.

[17] UNESCO, *World Directory of National Science Policy-Making Bodies*, Vol. 2 (1968), p. 66.
[18] The Ministry of Defence has absorbed such a large proportion of the country's scientific potential that a 1961 government-sponsored study of manpower problems concluded that the government 'should reappraise the present distribution of scientific talent under the control of the Ministry of Defence, including the Atomic Energy Commission, with an aim of determining whether significant gains could be made by reducing the scope and scale of government laboratories in favour of arrangements which rely more heavily on contracts with civilian institutions', Elie Ginzberg, *Report on Manpower Utilization in Israel* (Jerusalem: National Council for Research and Development, September (1961), p. 4.
[19] Beaton and Maddox, *op. cit.*, p. 23.
[20] 'Report of Secretary-General U Thant on the Effects of the Possible Use of Nuclear Weapons and on the Security and Economic Implications for States of the Acquisition and Further Development of These Weapons,' (10 October, 1967), in US Disarmament and Arms Control Agency, *Documents on Disarmament, 1967* (Washington, DC: Government Printing Office, 1968), p. 503. (Hereafter cited as *Thant Report.*)

THE NUCLEAR ESTABLISHMENT

ATOMIC POLICY-MAKING BODIES

Atomic Energy Commission: The beginnings of the AEC have already been discussed. The most significant developments since 1954 were the resignation *en masse* of its members in 1957 and its complete reorganization in April 1966, when it was attached to the Prime Minister's Office and the Premier himself assumed the chairmanship. The official justification for removing the AEC from the jurisdiction of the Defence Ministry was that the then Prime Minister, Levi Eshkol, had been in direct charge of the nuclear desalination project talks with the United States, and, since this was the most important long-range project in the atomic field, it was felt that decision-making in this sphere should be concentrated for better co-ordination and planning. Curiously enough, Eshkol was then Defence Minister as well and, traditionally, the two posts of Premier and Defence Chief had been held concurrently by the same person—a practice established by Ben-Gurion—which suggests that the AEC transfer actually aimed at limiting military influence on the programme by withdrawing it from the jurisdiction of the Defence Ministry. What is certain is that all decisions of importance in the Israeli nuclear establishment are now made by the highest political authority in the country. In other words, nuclear policy has become better integrated into the country's politico-military planning, and developments in the programme have come to reflect adopted policies more closely. The most important long-range practical consequence of this integration is that no serious gap is likely to develop between the tasks that the nuclear establishment may be called upon to fulfil by the leadership at a given moment, and its actual technological and plant capacity to 'deliver the goods'.

The ouster of Professor Bergmann from the AEC chairmanship ended a nine-year period (1957-66) throughout which the 'hawkish' orientation fostered by David Ben-Gurion and Shimon Peres in the nuclear field had been particularly pronounced. Bergmann had always been a 'Ben-Gurion-man', and his removal also probably reflected Prime Minister Eshkol's desire to reduce the behind-the-scenes influence of the former Premier, which had continued to be felt through the Defence Ministry—and its scientists—which he had long headed (1948-53, 1955-63). The leadership of the establishment was extricated from the hands of the military and taken over by the Premier in a deliberate attempt to give it, at least outwardly, a more civilian outlook. This shift was soon reflected in Eshkol's offer to President Johnson late in 1966 to freeze operations at the

Dimona plant at the point they had reached—reportedly in exchange for arms, a move that angered former Premier Ben-Gurion, Bergmann and other hard-liners.[21]

The offer in itself is interesting because it probably implies that original plans called for a more advanced nuclear set-up at Dimona than the one obtaining in 1966 and which has apparently remained the same to this day. The next logical addition to the fuel cycle is a plutonium reprocessing plant, and if earlier plans called for such a facility, this could be highly significant in terms of Israel's nuclear intentions.

With the reorganization of the AEC, its membership was increased to 17, personally appointed by the Prime Minister himself from among members of the universities and higher institutes, utility corporations, government ministries and public life, for a two-year term of office. It comprises four advisory sub-committees, *viz*, Research, Education and Manpower Training, Power and Water, and Radio-active Isotope Applications. Its budget is provided by the government and amounted to 43 million Israeli pounds in 1967-68.[22] Professor Israel Dostrovsky is its Director-General.

Israel is a member State of the International Atomic Energy Agency (IAEA) and voted in favour of its safeguards system in 1960. She has bilateral agreements for co-operation in the nuclear field with eight countries and exchange information agreements with 600 institutions in 80 countries 'on both sides of both the Iron Curtain and the Bamboo Curtain.'[23]

A very special connection naturally exists with the French Commissariat à l'Energie Atomique in view of the close co-operation in atomic matters between the two countries. Significantly, Israel is the only country to maintain a permanent liaison organ with the French Commissariat, and again the only one to have had a permanent mission at the French Ministry of National Defence. This relationship has been seriously impaired by the new orientation given to French policy towards the Middle East by General de Gaulle and pursued by his successor.

National Council for Research and Development: Established in February 1960 to replace the Scientific Research Council, this body

---

[21] Hodes, *op. cit.*, p. 6.
[22] *Jerusalem Post*, 16 August, 1968.
[23] Mordecai Moragh, Nahal Soreq Administrative Head, in *Jerusalem Post*, 16 August, 1968.

has principal responsibility for advising the government on science policy, both over-all and in detail, as well as for planning and co-ordinating the government's research effort. Its activities and decisions are therefore directly relevant to the nuclear programme insofar as it is entrusted with the task of determining the future shape and orientation of the country's scientific manpower, and developing its technological and industrial base. Among the functions assigned by the government to the Council are (a) to advise the government on action relating to scientific research and planning, and technological developments of national significance; (b) to make decisions as to the apportionment and utilization of the funds for research and development at the disposal of the government and its agencies; and (c) to initiate programmes for scientific research and technological development projects.[24] The Council thus has 'decisive influence on the character of science in Israel.'[25] Secret defence research, however, has been kept outside its jurisdiction. Its first chairman was IAEC Director-General Professor Dostrovsky. Its present chairman is Professor Eliezer Tal, also a member of the Atomic Energy Commission.

The Council operates several national laboratories, including the Negev Institute for Arid Zone Research at Beer-sheba, where investigations into sea-water desalination by various methods, including nuclear power, have been undertaken.[26] It has also launched an extensive campaign aimed at strengthening the industrial research sector, through grants and concerted projects with industry.[27] Industrial research remains the weak spot in the over-all Israeli scientific and technological effort, and this may have some detrimental effects on an eventual nuclear weapons programme, as will be seen.

THE MILITARY AND POLICY-MAKING

Though not strictly classifiable as a policy-making organ, the *Advisory Committee on General Research and Development* set up within the Ministry of Defence by Moshe Dayan in June 1968 to examine general principles for the direction of defence-oriented

---

[24] From the Cabinet decision of 15 November, 1959 as amended, in Israel Government, *National Science Policy and Organisation of Research in Israel* (Jerusalem: Prime Minister's Office, National Council for Research and Development, March 1969), p. 9.
[25] Israel Government, *Year Book: 1960/61*, p. 65.
[26] Tauber, *op. cit.*, p. 70.
[27] Zahlan, *op. cit.*, p. 132.

research, as well as initiate research or development projects, has a natural role to play in the determination of Israel's nuclear policy, primarily in its military aspects. One of the committee's tasks is to increase the number of engineers and scientists graduating in fields needed by the defence establishment. Professor E. D. Bergmann, who had been dismissed from the chairmanship of the Atomic Energy Commission in 1966, was appointed Co-ordinator, and Professor, Ephraim Katchalski Chairman. Both are, together with Professors Dostrovsky and Yiftah, among the key men of the atomic programme. Apart from being Chief Scientist at the Defence Ministry, Professor Katchalski has been the co-ordinator of the Israel-US sea-water desalination project and, of course, a long-standing member of the IAEC. Indeed, he provides an index of the way the close connection between the IAEC and the defence establishment underpins the whole Israeli nuclear effort.[28]

Further evidence of this link is provided by the fact that the actual construction of the two reactors and their annexes was undertaken by the Defence Department's *Scientific Development Projects Division*, whose 'principal assignments are to supply atomic research with the necessary apparatus, establish laboratories and ancillary installations, and staff and equip them.'[29] This organ is also represented on the IAEC and actually shares in the work of the committee in charge of the reactors, studies siting problems and has a say in the evaluation and choosing of reactor types.[30]

The intention here is not to evoke all sorts of sinister implications because they do not necessarily follow from the facts just mentioned. Here, the peculiar character of the Israeli defence set-up must be taken into account. Ever since the establishment of the State, the need to keep an abnormally large and sophisticated military machine has had to compete with the urgent economic requirements of the country for the limited resources available. The solution to this resource allocation dilemma has been 'to create a military estab-

[28] Professor Israel Dostrovsky provides another example of how a handful of leading scientists dominate the whole Israeli scientific-military complex (including the nuclear programme) at both the decision-making and execution stages. For a time, he held the following positions concurrently: Director-General of the IAEC, Chairman of the National Council for Research and Development, Director of the Scientific Development Projects Division at the Defence Ministry, and Head of the Isotopes Department at the Weizmann Institute.
[29] Israel Government, *Year Book: 1960/62*, p. 92.
[30] *Ibid.*, *1965/66*, pp. 83-84.

lishment that would provide maximal use of its technical and managerial skills at a minimal cost in manpower and funds.'[31] In other words, the Defence Ministry and the Army were entrusted with supplying services that would normally be provided by the civilian sector, not least among them being the manufacture of weapons and munitions, the assembling and servicing of aircraft, and research activities in several fields, such as rocketry and electronics, of military as well as civilian importance. An example of the high-quality research conducted at the Defence Ministry is provided by its *Research and Planning Department*, which concentrates its efforts in four main spheres: weapons planning, electronics, physics and chemistry. Some of the electronic instruments installed at the Dimona Plant were developed by this Department,[32] and since 1964 Israel has exported nuclear research equipment.[33]

Nonetheless, while the interdependence between the military and the atomic establishments in terms of institutional bodies, installations and personnel can partly be explained by the peculiar role of the military in the country's economic structure, the fact remains that Israel's nuclear establishment was set up and is being run and serviced by the military to all intents and purposes. Even though crucial decisions, such as the go-ahead to a weapons programme, will be made at the highest political level, there is no doubt that the pressures that can be exerted by military circles would be enormous, not only because of their influence and power in a 'nation in arms' such as Israel, but precisely because they have the largest share in the day-to-day running of the programme. Final decisions are not made in a vacuum; they are to a large extent pre-determined by the various givens of the situation. If a certain party has the opportunity to shape these givens and manipulate them with a view to influencing the final decision, the chances are that this decision will be a foregone conclusion that only awaits the proper setting and the opportune moment to crystallize into action. This 'stacking of the cards' in favour of a military nuclear orientation may be particularly decisive in the Israeli situation where 'a few vigorous ...

---

[31] J. C. Hurewitz, 'The Role of the Military in Society and Government in Israel,' in *The Military in the Middle East*, Sidney N. Fisher, ed., (Columbus, Ohio: Ohio State University Press, 1963), p. 94.

[32] Israel Government, *Year Book: 1959/60*, p. 180.

[33] *Kol-Ha'am* (Tel Aviv), 4 November, 1964. On Israel's military industry, see: 'Israel Aircraft Industries,' in *Interavia* (Geneva), March, 1968; 'Israel's Booming Arms Industry,' in the *Jewish Chronicle* (London), 29 November, 1968.

military leaders tend to exercise an undue influence on politico-military decisions' in a country that 'seems to have become a modern Sparta in its politico-military attitudes';[34] where, regardless of how opposed public opinion and a large segment of the political spectrum may be to nuclear weapons, no public debate—such as the recurring one in India, for example—that could provide a salutary counter-balancing effect is possible because of the paramount need for secrecy; where, moreover, all major steps in the nuclear field have been taken without the legislative's knowledge or approval; and where the same reduced and tightly knit group of political, military and scientific leaders who created and developed the nuclear option (at an expense of many hundreds of millions of dollars) over the years is apparently to decide whether and when that option is finally to be taken up.

Hence the importance of briefly examining the degree of influence traditionally exercised on the Israeli decision-making process at the highest level by the small group of individuals, both military and civilian, who as 'bearers of "security" values'[35]—to use Eisenstadt's phrase—have determined in large measure Israel's defence posture and strategy from the outset and continue to have a decisive say in all matters affecting the country's security and its military power.

Given the set of circumstances accompanying the creation of the Israeli state, namely, its establishment on a portion of Palestine in the face of the active hostility of the native population—which was partially evicted in the process—and against a background of military engagement with the surrounding countries ending in an uneasy truce and the perpetuation of this enmity through economic boycott, diplomatic ostracism and verbal menaces, the resultant security situation rendered the military's intervention in politics and decision-making unavoidable. Indeed, with the adoption of the 'Arab encirclement of Israel' doctrine by the leadership after 1949 and the institution of the policy of retaliation as a counter-measure, the Army's strategy came to 'determine to a large extent the course of

[34] US Congress, Senate Committee on Foreign Relations, *War or Peace in the Middle East?* Report by Senator Joseph S. Clark on Study Mission to Greece, United Arab Republic, Jordan and Israel, Committee Print, 90th Cong., 1st sess. (Washington, DC: Government Printing Office, 1967).
[35] S. N. Eisenstadt, *Israeli Society* (London: Weidenfeld and Nicolson, 1967), p. 325. This is a carefully-researched and comprehensive sociological study of the Jewish community in Palestine both before and after 1948.

Israel's foreign relations' as well.[36] In other words, since the strategy of across-the-border retaliation and constant preparedness made surprise and speed essential requirements, the formulation of defence policy and the timing of military action were perforce left completely in the hands of *Zahal* (acronym for Israel Defence Forces) and the Defence Minister. In actual terms, this was equivalent to leaving the political initiative as well to the military in so far as Israel's relations with the external world were concerned.

This situation was further aggravated by the practice of concentrating the premiership and the Defence ministry in the hands of one person, a concentration further accentuated by the fact that the Defence Minister is in fact the commander-in-chief of the armed forces as well.[37] David Ben-Gurion's emphasis on and active promotion of *Zahal* as the true and only representative of modern Israel whose 'moral structure and heroic role replaces the pioneer as the symbol of the ideal in the post-state era,'[38] as well as his almost exclusive concentration on foreign affairs and defence matters during his long tenure, greatly contributed to the growth in influence of the 'security' establishment.

Furthermore, the responsibility that, as mentioned earlier, devolved on the military regarding the production and supply of their own requirements in terms of arms and equipment resulted in the rapid development of an industrial and scientific empire based on the Ministry of Defence. In consequence, the military came to wield considerable power and pressure-potential as an important member of the industrial, scientific and educational sectors, thus gaining a large measure of control over the country's economy.[39]

In 1961, an attempt was made to limit the ascendancy of the military and their undue influence on the running of the country. The ability of the Defence Minister under Israeli law to take major

[36] Perlmutter, 'The Institutionalization of Civil-Military Relations in Israel,' p. 416. The theory of 'Arab Encirclement' was expounded by the then Chief-of-Staff General Moshe Dayan in 'Israel's Border and Security Problem,' *Foreign Affairs Vol.* XXXIII (January, 1955), pp. 250-63.

[37] See also Hurewitz, *Middle East Politics: The Military Dimension* (New York: Praeger for the Council on Foreign Relations, 1969), pp. 373-74.

[38] Perlmutter, 'The Institutionalization of Civil-Military Relations in Israel,' p. 425.

[39] The Ministry of Defence is the largest employer in the country. In 1966-67 defence expenditures accounted for 11 per cent of the GNP; by 1969-70, the percentage had jumped to 21 per cent, and was expected to reach 30 per cent in 1971. The budget devoted to secret defence-oriented research is assumed to be at least equal to total expenditure on scientific and technical research for civil purposes (I£ 146·6 million in 1966-67). See *National Science Policy and Organisation of Research in Israel*, p. 19.

policy decisions in the field of military affairs and security without prior cabinet consultation or Knesset authorization[40]—a prerogative that has been exercised on several occasions—has been a constant factor in Israeli politics that has sometimes led to crises such as the ever-recurring 'Lavon Affair'. After the Affair's last outburst in 1961, which led to the fall of Ben-Gurion's broad coalition government, the need to define once and for all the relationship between the military hierarchy and ultimate civilian control became evident, particularly to the opposition. A Ministerial Security Committee was set up by the new government in November 1961 which, in an advisory capacity, would have the right to request information and pass judgment on all aspects of security affairs including weapons development. The chairmanship of the Committee was however given to the Defence Minister, with wide prerogatives which were carefully protected. Moreover, control over military intelligence and matters that the country's security dictated should remain secret were safeguarded from access by the Committee, which was also expressly denied any policy-making authority.[41] In other words, the creation of this Committee did not provide the intended solution to the issue of civilian control over the military establishment. On the contrary, it provided evidence of the power and influence exercised by the Defence Ministry, and of the Mapai majority Party's readiness to tolerate this state of affairs, whose impact on the country's nuclear policies cannot but make itself felt in one way or another.

[40] Hurewitz, 'The Role of the Military in Society and Government in Israel,' p. 100.
[41] Halpern, 'The Military in Israel,' p. 356.

CHAPTER V

Future Developments: Nuclear Desalting

No survey of the Israeli nuclear programme would be complete without a brief discussion of the path future expansion in the field is likely to take. Existing plans for the future will be useful also in assessing the degree to which military considerations will influence the adoption of nuclear energy for 'peaceful purposes' beyond the present research stage and the extent of their contribution to a weapons option. Though recently there has been talk of erecting power reactors for electricity production, it is nuclear sea-water desalting that has engaged the thought and efforts of Israel's leaders since the idea was first mooted in 1963.

The most serious obstacles to Israel's development threatens to be the lack of sufficient water resources. Water is crucial for increasing the area of land available for settlement, which is still far smaller than the area of irrigable land. The solution of this problem is tightly connected with the absorptive capacity of the country, i.e. the ability to accept and settle Jewish immigrants, and its continued economic development. Both a significant and steady Jewish influx as well as economic prosperity are considered by the country's leadership to be essential requirements for long-term security. Studies made by Tahal (Water Planning for Israel, Ltd.) have demonstrated that by 1970 water consumption would have reached 90 per cent of potential resources; water conservation and reclamation projects not withstanding, a supplementary annual supply of 120 million cubic metres will be needed by the early 1970s.[1]

At the same time, power consumption forecasts predicted that total maximum demand for electricity would rise from 780 megawatts in 1966 to 1,630 megawatts in 1975. Moreover, by 1970 the

[1] *Engineering Feasibility and Economic Study for Dual-Purpose Electric Power-Water Desalting Plant for Israel* (Prepared for the United States-Israel Joint Board by Kaiser Engineers of Oakland, Cal., and Catalytic Construction Company of Philadelphia, Penn., USA, January 1966), p. 7 (Hereafter cited as *Kaiser Feasibility Study*.) This study has been revised twice since 1966.

56

doubling period of maximum demand would be eight years.[2] Taking into account these growth expectations and other factors such as production and operation costs, economies of scale, and increased efficiency, the Israel Electric Corporation determined that the optimum size of power plants to be built by the early 1970s to cope with such expansion would be in the range of 175-200 megawatts net.[3] Even larger plants were subsequently found to be suitable, partly because the above power forecasts were later proven conservative.

Given this situation, it was only natural for Israeli planners to find in dual-purpose nuclear-desalting plants the ideal solution to their worries, since these plants would produce electric power and desalt seawater at the same time. Atomic power-producing reactors have been under consideration by Israel since the mid-1950s. In a candid statement at the first Geneva 'Atoms for Peace' Conference held in August, 1955, that reflected concern at the vulnerability of the country's external fuel supplies, which come mostly from Iran, the Head of the Israeli delegation and Director General of the Foreign Ministry, Walter Eytan, threw light on Israel's plans:

> Israel has no fuel resources of her own. We cannot depend on outside fuel resources. In case of war, they can be cut off and the country's life could be brought to a halt. That is why we are making every effort to increase our own energy resources. We hope to have an atomic research pile built within the next four years.[4]

It became subsequently evident, however, that, to be economically justifiable, such plants had to produce between 500 and 1,000 megawatts of electricity, an output that Israel could not possibly absorb. Only if power production costs could be balanced off by substantial fresh water production, as was to be the case in the dual-purpose plants, would the project become feasible.

An index of the importance attached to nuclear desalting by the

---

[2] *Ibid.*, pp. 24-26. By 1968, installed generating capacity had reached 1008 megawatts. In December of the same year, the Israeli Electric Corporation decided to build two power stations at Ashdod of 214 megawatts each, to be conventionally fuelled; at least one would be ready by 1973, *Jerusalem Post*, 20 December, 1968.

[3] *Ibid.* See also, M. Nelken, 'Electric Power in Israel,' in International Atomic Energy Agency, *Small and Medium-Size Power Reactors*, Proceedings of a Panel, Vienna, 24-28 June, 1968 (Vienna: IAEA, 1969).

[4] *Jerusalem Post*, 11 August, 1955. Significantly, the statement was strongly denied by the Israeli Foreign Ministry a few days later, *ibid.*, 16 August, 1955.

Israeli Government is provided by the fact that the Prime Minister himself took direct charge of the matter when it came under renewed consideration in 1964 following President Johnson's proposal—made at a dinner of the American Committee for the Weizmann Institute in February—to aid Israel in the construction of one such plant.[5] The offer was made as Israel completed preparations to take water from Lake Tiberias and fears of an armed confrontation with the Arab States over this issue brought the water problems of the region to the fore, and it resulted in a decision by the two governments reached during Eshkol's visit to Washington in May of that year jointly to sponsor the Kaiser study.

This Israeli-US project has not been the only one under consideration for the area. Without going into a detailed account of all developments in this field, we can summarise them as follows:

Nuclear desalting for Israel has been approached on two levels: local and regional.

On the *local* level, the project in existence is that proposed by President Johnson. The most important developments to date have been the conclusion of the engineering feasibility study, the introduction of legislation in the American Congress early in 1969 aimed at authorizing aid for the construction of the plant, and the subsequent decision of the Nixon Administration not to press ahead with the project at the present time.

The feasibility study carried out in 1965 showed that a dual-purpose plant with a capacity of 200 megawatts (electrical) saleable power and 100 million gallons per day of desalted water was technically feasible.[6] Total estimated cost varied between $187 million at 5 per cent capital interest rate and $210 million at 10 per cent capital interest rate.[7] In 1967, further plans were made with a view to expanding power production to 300 megawatts, while water output would remain unchanged. The plant would not become operational before 1975.[8]

No major developments were registered from 1966 to 1968, while protracted negotiations and studies were carried on which, as will be seen, were essentially of a political rather than a technical nature, though they outwardly focused on the question of American financial and technical aid. The project finally seemed to get under way with the submission of legislation to Congress by out-going

[5] *New York Times*, 2 February, 1964.
[6] *Kaiser Feasibility Study*, p. 3.
[7] *Ibid.*, Table II, p. 6. At a 1965 exchange rate of $1 = I£3.
[8] *Jerusalem Post*, 15 November, 1967.

FUTURE DEVELOPMENTS

President Johnson on 17 January, 1969—four days before he left the White House—followed by the introduction of a similar bill in the House by a group of nine Congressmen on 23 January[9] which would authorize the United States government to

> enter into an agreement with the Government of Israel to provide financial, technical, and other assistance to the Government of Israel for the design, development, and construction of a dual-purpose nuclear electrical power generation and desalting plant in Israel. Such plant shall be designed to produce approximately one hundred million to one hundred and fifty million gallons of fresh water per day and approximately three hundred thousand to four hundred thousand kilowatts of electricity. The cost of such plant shall be shared by the United States and the Government of Israel with the United States share established by the President at an amount determined by him to be sufficient to reduce the cost of the water produced by such plant to a level which would make it economically feasible to use such water for agricultural and industrial purposes.[10]

The Johnson proposal called for American participation not exceeding $40 million over five years, which would cover half the cost of the desalting unit in the plant and operating expenses; an $18 million loan was also requested. This proposal was based on the optimistic results of the Kaiser study, which it took as its point of reference. However, such optimism has been proven ill-founded by several analyses and studies carried out subsequently,[11] which have demonstrated, among other things, that the cost of desalted water to the Israeli farmer will be much higher than calculated. Indeed, an Israeli water expert at the Ministry of Agriculture has concluded that 'there is no economic justification for the general widespread introduction of desalted water into agricultural use at the present time. As for the future, though the

[9] US Congress, House, *Congressional Record*, 23 January, 1969, p. H431 (Daily Digest).
[10] H.R. 4307, 91st Cong., 1st sess. (1969).
[11] See: W. E. Hoehn, *The Economics of Nuclear Reactors for Power and Desalting*, RM-5227-PR/ISA (Santa Monica, Calif., RAND Corp., 1967); P. Wolfowitz, *Middle East Nuclear Desalting: Economic and Political Considerations*, RM-6019-FF (Santa Monica, Calif., RAND Corp., 1969); Marion Clawson, Hans H. Landsberg, Lyle T. Alexander, 'Desalted Seawater for Agriculture: Is it Economic?' *Science* (Washington DC), CLXIV (6 June, 1969), pp. 1141-48.

huge atomic-powered plants planned promise a considerable reduction in costs, it is by no means a foregone conclusion that the
internal economies of scale will suffice to offset the very serious
costs associated with the mammoth size of plants'.[12] At this point,
the question of Israel's ulterior motives in pressing for a complex
that would tie-up enormous—and locally unavailable—capital and
produce water at uncompetitive prices inevitably comes to mind,
particularly in view of the curious timing of the Johnson Administration's move and the pressures exerted by pro-Israel circles in
Washington throughout 1969 to secure passage of the necessary
legislation.[13]

Such economic considerations obviously influenced the incoming
Nixon Government's decision, taken in the spring of 1969, to
eliminate the Johnson proposal from the budget. Other factors that
seem to have weighed as heavily are of a more political nature.
The White House made it known in September that it desired to
couple 'any agreement with Israel with some corresponding gesture
to friendly Arab nations hopefully to alleviate the refugee problem
which is causing instabilities in the Middle East'.[14] This was in
line with the new Administration's early policy of seeking a more
balanced approach to the Arab-Israeli question. The main American
reservation, however, was that which had also prevented the Johnson Government from acting on the project until the penultimate
hour, namely, the Israeli lack of responsiveness to American
insistence on surrender of the nuclear option in exchange for aid
towards the proposed dual-purpose plant. The enormous contribution that a large nuclear desalination plant would make to the
credibility and magnitude of an Israeli nuclear weapons stockpile,
particularly in view of regional developments since 1967, rendered
Washington's concern all the more urgent and its reluctance all
the more understandable.

This position remained unchanged in the face of an amendment
incorporated into the 1970 Foreign-Aid Bill in September by the

[12] E. Dlayahu, 'Economic Considerations in Introducing Desalted Water
Into Agricuture,' *Value to Agriculture of High-Quality Water From Nuclear
Desalination,* Reports of a Panel held in Vienna, 30 October-3 November,
1967.
[13] See for example the issues of 23 July, 6 August and 12 November of
Near East Report, the organ of the American-Israel Public Affairs Committee, a Zionist lobbying group.
[14] Letter from deputy presidential assistant William E. Timmons to Representative William F. Ryan, dated 13 September, 1969. Jewish Telegraphic
Agency (JTA) *Daily News Bulletin,* 19 September, 1969.

House Foreign Affairs Committee at Congressional initiative in lieu of the measure dropped by the Nixon Administration. The amendment, which contained the same terms as the Johnson proposal, was opposed by the Executive because 'the technology of water desalination has not yet advanced to the point that it would be sensible to invest a large amount of US and Israeli funds in a plant using the existing technology. The water produced by such a plant would be uneconomic in cost and require perpetual subsidies ... '[15] Significantly, the news agency report on the US decision carried under the same rubric the denial by Israeli Foreign Ministry officials that their government had been the subject of renewed pressures by Washington for Israeli subscription to the Non-Proliferation Treaty.[16]

On the *regional* level, a giant project was suggested in the summer of 1967 along the lines of an idea put forward by former President Eisenhower and former USAEC Chairman Admiral Strauss that envisaged the construction of several large nuclear desalting plants in the Middle East as a direct attack on what was considered to be the 'greatest bar to a long-term settlement' of the Arab-Israeli conflict: 'The chronic shortage of fresh water, useful work and an adequate food supply.'[17] It was thought that, by providing a solution to these pressing economic problems, this project would prepare the ground for a peacefully-negotiated settlement of the conflict, which had forcefully demonstrated a few months earlier what a threat it could be to world-wide security. The proposal was embodied in August, 1967 in US Senate Resolution 155, as follows:

> Whereas the security and national interests of the United States require that there be a stable and durable peace in the Middle East; and
>
> Whereas the greatest bar to a long-term settlement of the differences between the Arab and Israeli people is the chronic shortage of fresh water, useful work, and an adequate food supply; and
>
> Whereas the United States now has available the technology and the resources to alleviate these shortages and to provide a

[15] Dr John Hannah, US Agency for International Development Administrator, in testimony before the Senate Appropriations Committee, *Jerusalem Post*, 25 November, 1969; JTA *Daily News Bulletin*, 26 November, 1969.

[16] JTA, *ibid.*

[17] President Eisenhower outlined his idea in detail in an article which appeared in the *Reader's Digest* of June, 1968.

base for peaceful cooperation between the countries involved:
Now, therefore, be it

Resolved, That it is the sense of the Senate that the prompt
design, construction, and operation of nuclear desalting plants
will provide large quantities of fresh water to both Arab and
Israeli territories and, thereby, will result in—

(1) new jobs for the many refugees;

(2) an enormous increase in the agricultural productivity of
existing wastelands;

(3) a broad base for cooperation between the Israeli and
Arab Governments; and

(4) a further demonstration of the United States efforts to find
peaceful solutions to areas of conflict; and be it further

Resolved, That the President is requested to pursue these
objectives, as reflecting the sense of the Senate, within and outside
the United Nations and with all nations similarly minded as
being in the highest national interest of the United States.[18]

In brief, the project consisted in the construction of three large
plants, two on the Mediterranean coast of Israel and the third on
the Gulf of Aqaba, either in Israel or in Jordan. A 'non-national
third party,' in the form of an internationally financed public-private
corporation, would be in charge of the project, whose products
would be shared by the countries directly involved in the conflict,
and in the construction of which the displaced Palestinians would
be employed as a means of alleviating their plight. The refugees
would also benefit later on from the lands that would become
available for cultivation with the increase in water supply and from
the new industries that would be created.[19]

The required technical and economic feasibility studies for this
ambitious scheme were entrusted to the USAEC-sponsored Oak
Ridge National Laboratory (ORNL), which was already engaged
in exploring the field of agro-industrial complexes built around
dual-purpose nuclear plants. The theory behind these self-contained,
closed economies is that in areas where the need for water is
great but electricity requirements are not substantial—and this

---

[18] S. Res. 155, 90th Cong., 1st sess. (1967).

[19] US Senate, Committee on Foreign Relations, *Construction of Nuclear
Desalting Plants in the Middle East, Hearings,* before the Committee on
Foreign Relations, Senate, on S. Res. 155 (A Resolution to Express the Sense
of the Senate Concerning a Means Toward Achieving a Stable and Durable
Peace in the Middle East), 90th Cong., 1st sess., 1967, p. 3.

would be the case in developing regions where deserts predominate and industries are relatively scarce, such as the Middle East—the large amounts of cheap power produced for the desalting process would provide the basis for an agglomeration of industries producing selected chemicals and metals. Though 'water only' plants could be erected, this would appreciably increase the cost of desalted water—perhaps by one-third.[20]

While the first study conducted at Oak Ridge was of a general nature,[21] the US Atomic Energy Commission, partially in response to Senate Resolution 155, entrusted ORNL in June 1968 with the task of studying the applicability of the agro-industrial nuclear centre concept to the Middle East. A Middle East Study Group of experts was formed at that time which has since then sent visiting teams to the area. While the final report is expected to be completed during 1971, interim reports sound a rather pessimistic note regarding near prospects of viable agro-industrial complexes either on a regional basis or for the UAR or Israel alone, and suggest that 'alternatives to power-desalting projects may offer more immediate solutions to the problem of economic growth in the countries concerned. These include, the de-emphasis of agricultural expansion in Israel in favour of greater industrialization and better use of Nile water in Egypt.'[22] The point is made, however, that 'non-economic factors ... may justify nuclear desalting in the Middle East area.'[23]

As it has turned out, the future of both projects—the local Israeli and the regional—has hinged on their 'political' rather than on their 'technical' feasibility.

The Eisenhower plan, ambitious in its scope and no less far-reaching in its objectives, suffers from one decisive disability: its implementation depends on a prior political settlement that would make co-operation between Israel and its Arab neighbours possible. The 'base for peaceful co-operation' it is designed to create must already exist as a precondition for its practical execution. In fact, this proposal puts the cart before the horse. It also reveals a basic misconception of—or perhaps disregard for—the underlying causes

[20] J. A. Lane, 'US Studies on Agro-Industrial Complexes,' Paper presented at the International Survey Course on Economic and Technical Aspects of Nuclear Power, IAEA, Vienna, 1-12 September, 1969, p. 1 (mimeographed).
[21] See the final report, *Nuclear Energy Centers, Industrial and Agro-Industrial Complexes*, ORNL-4290, UC-80-Reactor Technology (Oak Ridge National Laboratory, Oak Ridge, Tenn., November 1968).
[22] Lane, *op. cit.*, p. 22.
[23] *Ibid.*

of the conflict, in that it conceives of them in essentially material-
istic terms, and attempts to defeat them by providing an 'economic'
solution that does not accord with the realities of the situation as
they are seen by at least one of the two contending sides. It is thus
not surprising that the project may have remained to this day a
mere 'expression of the sense of the Senate.' Its unworkability in
the present political context did not pass unperceived by the State
Department. In a letter to the Committee on Foreign Relations
outlining the Department's attitude to the project, Assistant Secretary Macomber sealed its fate with the following statement:

> We share your view that regional economic co-operation can
> advance the cause of peace, but we believe that effective economic
> co-operation between Israel and the Arab States will have to be
> founded on political understanding. Antagonisms are so deep-
> seated that we do not believe that hope of economic progress
> alone is enough to break the political deadlock. . . . In the absence
> of a political base, we believe it would be premature for the
> United States to press regional co-operation on Israel and the
> Arab States.[24]

While expressing its pessimism regarding the Eisenhower proposal, the State Department pointed out in its letter that bilateral
agreements were more realistic, and mentioned by way of example
the joint US-Israeli project. Yet, as pointed out, no positive results
have been achieved in this direction either, in spite of the encouraging conclusions reached by the Kaiser study. Moreover, recent
expansion work undertaken by Israel in conventional power stations
has been interpreted as signalling a postponement of nuclear power
production until at least the mid-1970s.[25]

The basic reason why this bilateral project has failed to materialize
is that the United States has made her financial and technical aid
conditional on Israel opening all her nuclear activities (meaning
Dimona) to international inspection.[26] Technically, it is very
doubtful whether her present know-how would enable Israel to

[24] US Senate *Hearings* on S. Res. 155, p. 33.
[25] *Jerusalem Post*, 18 August, 1967; 20 December, 1968.
[26] See: Nimrod, *op. cit.*, p. 907; Y.V., 'Atoms and a Middle East Tashkent,'
New Outlook (Tel Aviv), IX (March, 1966), pp. 3-6; George Quester, 'Israel
and the Nuclear Non-Proliferation Treaty,' *Bulletin of the Atomic Scientists*
(Chicago), XXV (June, 1969), p. 45. Prime Minister Meir acknowledged
that US cancellation of the project was not due to purely economic factors
in an interview with the *Jewish Chronicle*, 12 December, 1969.

dispense with American asistance in this advanced and as yet largely untested nuclear desalting technology. Financially, Israel's bargaining latitude is as limited. If the rate of interest paid on the large capital outlay the plant will require exceeds two per cent, the cost of water would become less advantageous than if other, non-nuclear methods were used. At the same time, it would be extremely difficult, if not impossible, to raise the necessary funds at such low interest rates, as attempts to obtain a West German loan had proved.[27] Taking advantage of this situation, the American Government has apparently sought to trade off its aid for an Israeli renunciation of the nuclear weapons option. That such conditions have been steadily refused is one clear indication of the importance assigned by Israel to keeping the nuclear alternative unimpaired.

The introduction of legislation in the Congress in January, 1969 by the Department of Interior enabling the American Government to extend the required financial and other aid may mean that the American conditions had finally been dropped by the Johnson Administration. In such case, Israel would have been within a few years in possession of a nuclear power-reactor with a rating of some 350 megawatts electrical. As a rule, every megawatt electrical will produce one kilogramme of plutonium per year. The envisaged desalting plant would then provide, as a by-product, some 350 kilogrammes of plutonium annually, or enough for 70 bombs in the 20-kiloton range.

The availability of this large plutonium output for military purposes is the more relevant aspect of the nuclear desalting projects from the point of view of this study. If the United States is to provide substantial aid, whether in the form of grants or minimal interest rates, she will no doubt apply proper safeguards on the uranium fuel she will supply and, in consequence, on the plutonium produced as a by-product. Even supposing that the United States will not insist on herself supplying the fuel, which is most improbable, alternative suppliers who would not require controls would be extremely difficult to find in view of the fact that the plant envisaged by the Israel-US team would use fuel enriched to three per cent in its U-235 isotope content.[28] Enrichment plants are possessed by the

---

[27] The Economist Intelligence Unit, *Quarterly Economic Review: Israel* (London), September, 1965, p. 11. Locally, even at an interest rate of 11 per cent, the maximum legally permitted, the demand for loans is usually greater than can be supplied, *ibid.*, annual supplement, 1966 (cited by Wolfowitz, *op. cit.*).
[28] *Kaiser Feasibility Study*, p. 137.

five nuclear powers only, none of which is likely to encourage an Israeli nuclear weapons programme however indirectly by supplying control-free enriched uranium.

Granting that the desalting plant may eventually be built and made subject to American or IAEA supervision there remains the possibility that whatever safeguards may be imposed could be evaded, and the fissile by-product could become available for weapons either through clandestine diversion, or through denunciation of existing agreements. Diversion might be feasible due to the large quantities involved. The studies made jointly by Israeli and American teams assumed ownership of the fuel materials by the Israeli Government throughout the fuel cycle, including the separated plutonium end-product.[29] Subject to an undertaking not to divert it to non-peaceful uses, Israel, as the owner of the plutonium, would have the right to stockpile it under her direct jurisdiction. She could then proceed to diverting small but significant quantities without undue risk of detection.[30]

A more effective alternative would be the unilateral denunciation of international commitments if the Israeli Government were to decide that circumstances dictate such a course of action. This problem of unilateral termination of agreements has not been given proper attention,[31] and existing safeguards systems (Euratom, European Nuclear Energy Agency, International Atomic Energy Agency, and US Atomic Energy Commission—i.e., bilateral agreements) do not prescribe any adequate penalties for such a contingency, the only really adequate deterrent being the threat of direct military or police action. Any measures short of forceful intervention would be insufficient to convince a country that feels the need to develop a nuclear capacity, and possesses a large stock of plutonium acquired and maintained at considerable expense, that it should make do with conventional weapons by virtue of an undertaking made under different conditions. States have never acted with such altruism whenever they felt their vital interests were at stake, and they are not likely to mend their ways overnight. As it has been pointed out, 'a decision to produce nuclear weapons is a major choice for any government. Even if it has no other

---

[29] *Ibid.*, p. 135.

[30] It has been pointed out that, if a two per cent range of error in fuel computation is inevitable, Israel could divert one per cent clandestinely and thereby accumulate a significant stockpile, Quester, *op. cit.*, p. 45.

[31] See Lewis C. Bohn, 'Atoms for Peace and Atoms for War,' *Disarmament and Arms Control*, III (Spring, 1965); Leonard Beaton, 'Nuclear Fuel-for-All,' *Foreign Affairs*, XLV (July, 1967).

implicatons, it will certainly cost large sums of money. Such a decision will be taken only because there is a strong conviction that it is necessary. A safeguards system which rests on the premise that governments possessing this conviction will nevertheless abandon their plans because of an inspection agreement made ten, twenty or thirty years before is out of touch with political reality.'[32]

Even the possibility of facing a fuel cut-off as a result of such a unilateral step, with the consequent losses for an industry and agriculture that would be geared to the plant's expected power and water production, would not prevent the Israeli Government from going ahead with its plans. Firstly, experience indicates that outside political opposition to nuclear spread in any one particular case will cease when the inevitability of such a development becomes evident. At this point, commercial considerations will become uppermost, and priority will be assigned to securing maximum profits by supplying the new 'nuclear power' with the expensive items its burgeoning programme will require.[33] Secondly, if research is maintained at its present rate, the development of a relatively cheap uranium enriching process through the gaseous centrifuge method will, by the mid-1970s, probably put small countries such as Israel in a position to have their own enrichment plants.[34] If this is coupled with an increase in local natural uranium production, which is envisaged by Israeli planners,[35] the fuel requirements of the desalting plant could then be locally provided. The far-reaching military implications of the self-sufficiency and independence in the nuclear field that Israel would thus acquire need no elaboration.

Having in mind considerations similar to those just outlined, the Nixon Administration is obviously inclined to refrain from financing or otherwise co-operating in the desalting project for as long as Israel's stand remains unchanged. If they feel able to solve locally the considerable technical difficulties involved, the Israelis might then presumably renew their attempts to obtain financial aid from other sources, which, being less concerned than the American Government with avoiding nuclear proliferation and less affluent, would presumably have no similar compulsions but would be interested in making a sound and profitable investment.

As pointed out, the economic feasibility of the project from the Israeli point of view has mainly depended on the interest rate at

[32] Beaton, 'Nuclear Fuel-for-All,' p. 664.
[33] Beaton, *Must the Bomb Spread?*, p. 44.
[34] See Chapter VI.
[35] See Chapter VII.

which the necessary capital could be obtained. In fixing maximum rates that could be paid without the water and power price becoming prohibitive to the local customer, purely financial factors were taken into account and the ceiling was set at 2 per cent.[36] This would be much too low a rate of interest to attract foreign capital. However, if the acquisition of a plutonium stockpile is assigned primary importance, i.e., if military considerations come to figure prominently in the calculations of the decision-makers, the interest rate they will be ready to pay would thereby cease to be determined by purely financial considerations. In other words, the Israeli Government would be willing to pay an interest rate which is directly proportional to the importance it assigns to plutonium possession. The keener it is on developing a military option, the more it will be willing to pay for its plutonium-producing installations.

On this basis, it can be assumed that, when Israel eventually concludes an agreement for the construction of her desalting plant, the financial terms of such agreement may provide at least a measure, if not a clear indication, of her interest in acquiring a substantial reserve of fissile material, and this in turn will aid in better evaluating her nuclear intentions.

[36] In 1966, it was calculated that, on a 2 per cent interest rate, the cost of one cubic meter of water would be 22·8 agorot (100 agorot = I£1); on a 5 per cent rate, the cost would rise to 53·4 agorot. The Israeli Water Authority was then distributing water at about 20 agorot per cubic meter. *Quarterly Economic Review: Israel*, May, 1966, p. 9.

PART II

The Military Option

CHAPTER VI

The Requirements of Weapons Production

THE process leading to the acquisition of nuclear weapons can be divided into three main parts:

(a) Production of the fissile core;
(b) Weapon design and assembly;
(c) Testing.

This is as far as the technical requirements are concerned. To them must be added the financial requisites, which are certainly crucial in determining the size of the programme and its scope.

These different requirements will be discussed below in a general way, while relating them to the existing Israeli set-up which has been already described.

PRODUCTION OF THE FISSILE CORE

In the most general terms, an atomic bomb is composed of a core of fissile material—uranium^{235} or plutonium^{239}—large enough to attain criticality but kept in a subcritical configuration until the time of the explosion.[1] A critical mass is the minimum amount of fissile material required in a particular configuration to sustain the chain reaction. If the critical mass is left 'uncontrolled', the reaction will take place at a very high speed and the mass will explode instantaneously, releasing vast amounts of energy. The function of a reactor is to control, i.e., slow down, the chain reaction and make available the energy released and other products of nuclear fission.

Uranium^{235}

It is found in a proportion of 0·7 per cent in natural uranium (the

---

[1] Uranium^{233}, obtainable from thorium in a reactor, is theoretically of use as a military explosive too. Up to this date, however, it has not been used by the nuclear powers and, at any rate, would have to be manufactured by using other fissile materials such as plutonium, which itself can be used to make weapons. This means that U-233 would not be available as a first step in a nuclear weapons programme.

remaining 99·3 per cent being the non-fissile isotope U-238), and to be useful for weapons it must be concentrated to over 90 per cent. So far, this has been done on a large scale only through an enormously expensive method, gaseous diffusion, which consists in turning the natural uranium metal into a highly corrosive hot gaseous compound (uranium hexafluoride) which is then made to pass through thousands of specially made porous membranes for months on end. The gas is pumped against the membranes, which contain millions of microscopic holes through which the lighter U-235 molecules tend to pass more easily than the heavier U-238 molecules, which are gradually left behind. This continues until the concentration of U-235 has reached the desired level. The gas is recycled as many as fifty times in order to avoid high wastage of uranium. About 4,000 stages are involved in each cycle, and each stage requires a pump facility and sizable porous membranes. Also, refined methods of automatic production control are required, as the process cannot be manually operated.

The whole operation is electrically powered and the amounts of electricity required are simply staggering. When running at full power, the three American gaseous diffusion plants are calculated to consume 6,000 megawatts per year, at a cost of $205,000,000. For the sake of comparison, consider that Israel's total generating capacity at the end of 1967 stood at 1,008 megawatts and is expected to reach 1446 megawatts by 1972.[2] A gaseous diffusion plant tailored to Israel's needs would certainly be much smaller than the American ones (which entailed an initial investment of $2,300,000,000), but this would not render the task substantially easier, as it has been found that 'the simplest possible design of a gas-diffusion plant consists of such a great number of individual high-grade components that high initial capital investments for even a minimum size installation are unavoidable.'[3]

No further details are necessary to lead to the conclusion that gaseous diffusion is beyond the capabilities of countries even much richer than Israel in financial and natural resources. Technological difficulties also loom large. This enrichment method has been qualified as the most difficult and demanding industrial process there is, and important information remains classified.

An alternative way for the obtainment of uranium[235] has been

---

[2] Nelken, op. cit., p. 126 (table IV).
[3] Christoph Hohenemser, 'The Nth Country Problem Today,' in Seymour Melman, ed., Disarmament: Its Politics and Economics, (Boston: The American Academy of Arts and Sciences, 1962), p. 245.

gradually developing during the last decade which might make it possible for countries as small as Israel to develop a weapons programme based on this explosive. This process, known as the gas-centrifuge method on isotope separation, opens such prospects because it appears to be much less expensive than gaseous diffusion. It is widely believed that a breakthrough in this area might provide great incentive to the nuclear spread, which prompted the United States in 1961 to classify all information on the process and to request West Germany and the Netherlands, whose scientists were working along parallel lines, to do the same. Britain was already applying similar restrictions. Japan and Australia are two other countries where considerable research on this procedure has been conducted.

The principle on which this method of separation is based is that molecules having different mass weights, such as those of uranium^{235} and uranium^{238}, tend to separate under the effect of the earth's gravitational field, and this separation occurs with an efficiency that is directly proportional to the strength of the gravitational field. Since very strong artificial fields can be created by rotating a drum around its axis at sufficiently high speeds, it was found that the centrifugal forces produced by such rotation would concentrate the lighter molecules—U-235 in this case—on the perimeter of the rotor.[4] A facility of this type might consist of a cascade made up of about ten stages of rotating machines, with about a thousand machines in the first stage, a number which would decrease gradually, thus concentrating the separated product.[5] The machines would have to spin at a speed of 50,000 to 100,000 revolutions per minute in order to develop centrifugal forces of about one million times gravity needed to separate the two uranium isotopes effectively.

The Netherlands claims to be ahead of both Britain and Germany in centrifuge technology.[6] A tripartite agreement was signed in March 1970 between these countries that provides for the pooling of know-how in a joint development of this enrichment process and its commercial exploitation. The construction of prototype plants in Britain (Capenhurst) and Holland (Almelo) has been started, and

---

[4] See J. Beckman, 'Gas Centrifuges for Cheaper Isotope Separation,' in C. F. Barnaby, ed., *Preventing the Spread of Nuclear Weapons* (London: Souvenir Press for the Pugwash Movement, 1969), for a recent report on the state of the art.

[5] Hohenemser, *op. cit.*, p. 247.

[6] David Fishlock, 'UK Coup in Centrifuge Deal,' *Financial Times* (London), 23 March, 1970.

the first stage of the British facility is expected to become operational in 1972.

As far as costs are concerned, the importance of this method lies not only in the fact that because of its smaller power and unit requirements it is intrinsically cheaper than the diffusion process, but also because the more improvements are introduced into the metals and equipment involved, the cheaper it will become. In other words, gas centrifuges are today limited in size and speed of rotation by the properties of available metal alloys.

> The enrichment attainable by a centrifuge varies with the fourth power of the rotor peripheral velocity. Therefore, small increases in rotor speed imply large increases in separative power.... An increase of 10 per cent in rotor speed may allow the elimination of one or two stages of a typical cascade and lower the number of machines required for a given production by a factor of 10. It is therefore clear that the cost of operation is very sensitive to the future development of special materials for centrifuge rotors. The development of such materials is a typical example of a problem that has no immediate theoretical limitation, and is almost certainly going to be solved with sufficient effort.[7]

When these words were written, five years were deemed necessary for research to cope with these technological problems,[8] which placed the probable date for a breakthrough in the late 1960s. The recent spate of reports, meetings, co-operation agreements and other related activities in Western Europe would seem to indicate that such a breakthrough has been achieved.

The principal advantages of the centrifuge method are: firstly, capital and running costs are much lower than for the diffusion process, mainly due to greatly reduced power consumption;[9] secondly, a centrifuge plant would be relatively easy to conceal, not only because of the lower power consumption but also because the installations would not be as easily identifiable as diffusion plants or plutonium-producing reactors, i.e., a weapons programme could be carried out in secret; thirdly, a U-235 based programme

---

[7] Hohenemser, op. cit., p. 247.

[8] Beaton and Maddox, op. cit., p. 8.

[9] Beckman mentions reductions of one order of magnitude in capital costs and five orders of magnitude in running expenses as compared with the diffusion process for quantities up to 100 Kg of separated U^{235} per year, op. cit., p. 97.

would open the way to the production of thermonuclear weapons, which are not more expensive than nuclear devices but need a U-235 trigger: theoretically, a plutonium trigger would be as adequate, but in practice, this has been found to be not only difficult to perfect but also less practical and costlier; and fourthly, a centrifuge plant can be built on a limited scale and can thus be adapted to the needs of a modest weapons programme.

The crucial question for Israel, however, is not whether she can master a centrifuge-based process which would be much cheaper than gaseous diffusion, but whether it is advisable to embark on a uranium-based programme at all when an even cheaper alternative is available through plutonium. Though uranium^{235} has its obvious advantages, primarily in relation to a thermonuclear weapons option, these have to be balanced against the financial attractiveness of acquiring a plutonium stockpile as a *by-product* of power-producing plants for which Israel stands in future need regardless of military considerations, both for the sake of electric power for her industries and of water for development and agriculture. In a reduced area such as the Middle East, with its population concentrations and absence of sophisticated defence systems, a thermonuclear arsenal is not an essential strategic requirement. On the contrary, the smallness of the area might make a thermonuclear threat lose much of its credibility.

Plutonium

Plutonium is an element not found in nature, but is produced from the irradiation of uranium in a reactor. The process that takes place can be summarized as follows: some of the uranium^{238} isotopes, which form the bulk of the natural uranium used as fuel, absorb neutrons released by the fissile uranium^{235} and become neptunium^{239} after about a half-hour; this element, which is highly unstable, decays within a period of two days into plutonium^{239}.

Since plutonium^{239} is an element totally different from uranium^{238}, with different chemical properties, it is relatively easy to separate the two elements in a chemical separation plant, obtaining as a result pure fissionable material useful as an explosive. Up to a few years ago, it was thought that plutonium^{240}, into which plutonium^{239} degenerates if left long enough inside the reactor, was not weapons-grade, and that, consequently, it would be necessary to run the reactors for short fuel cycles of one or two months' duration, after which time the spent fuel elements would have to be recovered in order to obtain Pu-239. Since the economical operation of a power reactor usually entails fuel cycles of from two to three years,[10] this was considered to be an important barrier in the way of small, not-so-rich countries wishing to acquire weapons-grade plutonium, as well as a fortunate technological fact that would make it relatively easy to establish an effective safeguards method. This would consist in simply monitoring the length of fuel-cycles, or alternatively adding the 'denaturant' Pu-240 to existing stockpiles of Pu-239. More recent evidence, however, suggests that Pu-240, which creates problems in weapons by its tendency to fission spontaneously thereby releasing stray neutrons which may pre-detonate the charge and reduce the explosive yield of the bomb in varying degrees, is liable to cause nuisances in some bomb designs but not in others, and the problem can be circumvented by advanced technologies without much difficulty. This has led to the scrapping of the 'denaturant' approach and the consideration of all plutonium as fit for utilization in nuclear weapons, at least in relation to safeguards procedures.[11]

The plutonium that has been fabricated by the reactor is not at this stage yet available for use in weapons. After a period of irradiation, the fuel elements become a mixture of fissionable materials—plutonium—and other fission products such as cesium and strontium, besides, the waste uranium. To obtain pure plutonium, these elements must be reprocessed in a chemical separation plant, from which the fissile material comes out ready for insertion in an explosive device.

Chemical separation facilities are very few outside the territory of the nuclear powers; only two are today in operation, one in India and one in Mol, Belgium, which is owned by a consortium of thirteen European countries (European Nuclear Energy Agency). The technology involved in their construction and operation has remained largely secret. This is due to the fact that they are intimately bound to military considerations, since they have no place in a peaceful nuclear programme, except perhaps to provide fuel for breeder reactors[12] and in the case of extensive set-ups where the

[10] Hohenemser, op. cit., p. 244.

[11] Arnold Kramish, The Peaceful Atom in Foreign Policy (New York: Harper & Row for the Council on Foreign Relations, 1963), pp. 24-25.

[12] A 'breeder' is an advanced type of reactor with a pure U-235 or plutonium fuel core which is very compact and at a high density of power. The neutron flow is so intense that, beside keeping the reaction going, large numbers of neutrons will bombard uranium or thorium 'blankets' surrounding the core, with the result that more fissionable material will be created than is burnt in the process.

scale of uranium reprocessing required would economically warrant building local facilities instead of relying on existing separation plants abroad. The high level of radiation present when the fuel rods are extracted from the reactor makes it necessary for re-processing plants to be operated automatically; only a few millionths of a gramme of plutonium can be absorbed by the human body with-out serious hazard.[13] The elaborate techniques required add to the cost of these facilities. On the other hand, the Indian experience suggests that if the technical know-how is available, the procure-ment of the required instrumentation and special equipment on the international market is feasible and the acquisition of a separa-tion plant would not present any unsurmountable difficulties.

From a security point of view, these plants are very difficult to dissimulate. Their typical long, tall, windowless shape, as well as their isolation from populated areas and other characteristic features will give them easily away to the trained eye, not to mention satel-lites fitted with cameras or 'spy-planes'. This factor may have played a role in delaying an Israeli decision to build such a plant. As the chairman of the US Atomic Energy Commission, Dr Glenn Seaborg, has asserted, however, it is not impossible to construct one in secret, particularly if it is designed to handle small quantities of spent fuel.[14]

In short, an independent and complete plutonium-producing complex, such as Israel would require if she desired to base a weapons programme on her locally extracted uranium or on im-ported ore, would entail the following installations: a plant for the concentration and refinement of the ore; one for the preparation of fuel elements, i.e., the conditioning of the uranium metal for use in the reactor; a nuclear reactor; and a chemical separation plant for plutonium extraction. To these must be added different servic-ing facilities essential for advanced and delicate processes of this nature, and, of course, a sufficient supply of heavy water must be secured.

As far as the Israeli programme stands at present, available evidence indicates that it has travelled all the stages along this road except the last: apparently, a chemical separation plant has not been built. As we have already pointed out, the construction of

[13] Kramish, *op. cit.*, p. 22.
[14] US Congress, Joint Committee on Atomic Energy, *Nonproliferation of Nuclear Weapons, Hearings* on S. Res. 179. 23 February, 1 and 7 March, 1966. 89th Cong., 2nd Sess. (Washington, DC: Government Printing Office, 1966), pp. 61-62. See also Beaton, *Must the Bomb Spread?*, p. 80.

such a facility in the absence of a breeder-reactor programme or a large nuclear establishment can be interpreted only in terms of a military capability, particularly in the tense political context of the Middle East. It is therefore possible that Israel may have built one in absolute secrecy so as not to alarm the Arabs into actively seeking a nuclear capability of their own. This is deemed rather unlikely, however, in view of the political consequences its discovery would probably entail, particularly since the Arab countries are not the only ones on the lookout. The Super-powers themselves are extremely concerned at the effects that an Israeli bomb would have on the problem of proliferation, apart from its possible consequences in the context of the Arab-Israeli dispute. It is felt that if a small country such as Israel attains nuclear status, considerations of prestige if nothing else would impel the group of industrialized and developed medium Powers that today stand undecided as to their nuclear future to follow the same road. American concern has particularly been put in evidence by Washington's insistence on obtaining access to Dimona and its attempts to open the whole Israeli programme to inspection in exchange for aid in the construction of nuclear desalting plants.

Occasional reports have suggested that the Dimona agreement with France may have provided for plutonium separation at the French facility, in which case Israel would be in possession of a stockpile of weapons-grade separated plutonium. Though the original arrangement could have contained such stipulations, it is most unlikely that they have been acted upon in view of the marked change in French policy towards the Middle East, which has been particularly manifest in the armaments field and had already set in by the time the Dimona reactor produced its first plutonium yield.

While bearing all this in mind, it must be observed that a separation plant can be built in a short time if a crash programme is undertaken, and that Israel has already moved in that direction with her 'hot laboratories' work.[15] An idea of the time-scale involved is provided by the Indian experience; the small facility at Trombay, which can reportedly reprocess up to 30 tons of uranium annually, took slightly less than three years to build.

---

[15] Beaton has suggested that an amount of plutonium sufficient for one bomb may have been separated in these laboratories, 'Why Israel Does not Need the Bomb,' *New Middle East* (London), No. 7, April 1969, pp. 7-11.

WEAPON DESIGN AND ASSEMBLY

Most technical information required for designing and constructing primitive atomic devices is in the public domain. Basic data, including primitive weapon designs, has been released with increasing liberalism by the United States Government ever since the 'Atoms for Peace' programme was launched in 1954-55. Of particular importance is published information on the physics of breeder, or 'fast,' reactors, which perform very much like a bomb. The considerable interest shown by Israeli scientists in breeder reactor technology is significant in this context.

The main design problem is connected with the 'fuse' that sets off the nuclear device. First-generation plutonium bombs have been generally exploded by a charge of chemical explosives that blasts the plutonium core inwards at a speed and in a manner such as to trigger off a chain reaction. Though substantial information on 'implosion' techniques has been published, continuous and intensive research must be carried out at all stages of the process to fill in gaps, and experiments must be conducted to adapt methods and designs to the particular grade of plutonium that the country has acquired. No amount of published material can be sufficient to enable a country to dispense completely with research in this area. Nonetheless, 'it is possible to gather from available sources full information about the methods which are best followed at various stages of the manufacture of atomic weapons [and] information about the actual operation of these processes is detailed enough to be able to specify the degree of efficiency which must be aimed at during the various stages of weapons manufacture.'[16]

TESTING

In general terms, testing of a nuclear device is no longer considered as absolutely necessary before deployment, particularly if it has been designed and assembled along conventional lines, without any essential innovations. The fact that the first primitive tests conducted by the nuclear powers did not fail, and that the first bomb ever used in actual warfare (Hiroshima) was not pre-tested, lend strength to this view. Moreover, a device is made up of several components, of which only one, the fissionable core, is nuclear, and all non-nuclear components can be tested in the laboratory or, as in

[16] Beaton and Maddox, *op. cit.*, p. 11.

the case of the implosion trigger, in conventional weapons test ranges.

The issue of whether a country is to test or not, however, cannot be meaningfully discussed without taking into account the country's particular nuclear aims and the geo-political context in which it finds itself at the time of decision. Thus, no one answer can be given that will be invariably suitable. For some countries, testing may be called for not so much as a technical necessity but for political ends, such as claiming the prerogatives that nuclear status confers, or demonstrating to a potential enemy that aggression will not pay, or even cowing neighbouring states into subservience. For others, circumspection may be held as an advantage, or even as absolutely essential for their security. Such may be the case for Israel, for the following reasons:

Firstly, showing her Arab neighbours that she has developed a nuclear capability will lead them to seek to redress the balance of forces whether through self-help, foreign assistance or international guarantees, which might cancel out most benefits she was seeking to obtain, and probably leave her in a weaker strategic position than before;

Secondly, she does not possess tracts of uninhabited territory within her boundaries large enough to conduct atmospheric tests without some risk of dangerous radioactive contamination. Moreover, atmospheric testing would involve a violation of the 1963 Nuclear Test-Ban Treaty to which Israel is a party. The alternative would be to test underground, which could be very expensive and carry a considerable risk of detection. The financial factor itself might make testing an unwarranted luxury, at least in the initial stages while only primitive devices following conventional designs are being produced, as the cost of constructing and instrumenting a testing site is calculated by some experts to amount to $75 million.[17]

Thirdly, even a single test would deprive Israel of a considerable portion of her weapon stockpile. The Dimona reactor has been yielding sufficient plutonium for one 20-kiloton bomb per year

---

[17] Beaton, 'Capabilities of Non-Nuclear Powers,' in Alastair Buchan, ed., *A World of Nuclear Powers?* (Englewoods Cliffs, NJ: Prentice-Hall, Inc. for the American Assembly, Columbia University, 1966), p. 32. A Swedish study made in 1967, however, put the total costs of one underground test of a 20-kiloton device at $12m., *Thant Report*, p. 500. Instrumentation in this case would presumably be minimal, which would severely limit the amount of valuable data that can be collected.

since 1966.[18] Even if no part of this yield were being used for research and other purposes, and were all being devoted to weapon production, Israel would not have more than four or five bombs by the early 1970s. Each test explosion would mean wasting away a full year's effort.

Fourthly, in view of super-power and international concern with the problem of proliferation, the disclosure of a weapons capability through testing would entail for Israel not only the disadvantages first mentioned above but also the strong disapproval of countries on which she depends in no small degree for her economic survival and continued existence as a viable state. The political cost would not be commensurate with the advantages derived from testing.

Fifthly, international disapproval and pressures applied by the super-powers may seriously threaten Israel's foreign sources of uranium metal. Of course, this would be an effective deterrent only if she decides to rely partially on imported fuel instead of seeking self-sufficiency by stepping up local production.

All this does not invalidate the fact that if Israeli scientists and the military deem it essential to test their devices and a way can be found to do it in secret, they will probably not hesitate to confront the heavy financial and other burdens involved. This would be particularly true if they decided to develop sophisticated bombs small and light enough to be used as warheads on the medium-range guided missiles Israel has been developing in France at an investment that in 1968 had already passed the $100 million mark.[19] An interesting piece of news in this connection is that released by the Pentagon shortly after the Hattiesburg test on 3 December, 1966, to the effect that, if decoupled, a test conducted at a depth of 1,100 metres underground would not be detected. Decoupling is the suspension of the device in an underground cavity surrounded by air, which acts as a cushion by absorbing the major seismic effects of the explosion. The larger the cavity, the stronger the explosion that can pass undetected: a 10-kiloton blast would require a cavity some 120 metres in diameter, and a 100-kiloton one of some 256 metres. Decoupling could take place closer to the surface as well, but then the cavity would have to be larger.[20]

This technique would open the possibility of carrying out tests in central Sinai, for example, without fear of detection.

[18] See Chapter VII.
[19] International Herald Tribune (Paris), 25 April, 1968.
[20] Le Monde (Paris), 9 January, 1967. Business Week (New York), 14 January, 1967, p. 8.

THE FINANCIAL REQUIREMENTS

The cost of a small weapons programme of the magnitude that is within Israel's present capability, i.e., a programme for the production of one, or at most two, 20-kiloton bombs a year, is, according to the latest estimates, well within that country's financial resources.

A study undertaken in 1967 by 12 experts from different countries at the request of the United Nations General Assembly revealed that a minimum programme consisted of ten 20-kiloton devices produced at the rate of one device per year would cost an estimated $104 million spread over ten years. Most of this capital would have to be invested in the earlier stages. This figure was broken down as follows:

	($ in millions)
Fissile material	70·0
Design and manufacture	18·0
Testing	12·0
Storage, maintenance	4·0
	104·0[21]

The cost per bomb would thus be 104/10=$10·4m.

The total figure seems rather low when compared with other estimates, one of which mentions $200 million as the 'basic costs in producing a bomb' and reaches this figure as follows:

	($ in millions)
Uranium refining, reactor and plutonium separation	100·0
Bomb design and production	25·0
Test range	75·0
	200·0[22]

It should be kept in mind, however, that these experts avowedly

[21] *Thant Report*, p. 500.
[22] Beaton, 'Capabilities of Non-Nuclear Powers,' p. 32.

based their estimates on countries possessing developed scientific, technical and industrial capabilities. They considered 'scientific and technical' capability to involve the availability of a sufficiently large corps of physicists, chemists, metallurgists, engineers, electricians, chemical plant operators and many other technicians 'essential for manufacture and assembly of components to the scientific specifications,' while 'industrial capability' was measured in terms of a country's 'established experience in fields of advanced technology, such as nuclear energy, aviation, electronics and space technology.'[23]

In Israel's case, though she possesses considerable scientific and technological potential that would fulfil the requirements, her industrial base is not yet developed to the point where she could sustain a nuclear development programme at the minimum costs envisaged in the Thant Report. Industry has lagged behind science, and concern at the existence of this lag has been repeatedly voiced. In November 1968, for example, Michael Tzour, a former Director General of the Ministry of Commerce and Industry, complained in an address to the Israel Management Institute and the Engineer's Association in Jerusalem that scientific innovations and discoveries are not finding the engineering companies and industrial research that will turn them into 'equipment that manufacturers can use,' and qualified industrial research as 'poor in Israel'.[24] A similar complaint has been more recently voiced by the Chief Scientist of the Defence Ministry, Dr Ephraim Katchalski. In 1962-65, expenditure by industry on scientific and technical research was in the range of 5 to 7 per cent, and rose to 10·6 per cent in 1966. In contrast, 60 to 70 per cent of total research funds went to institutions of higher learning.[25] Out of an estimated government expenditure of I£250m. on scientific research during 1969 in both the civilian and military spheres, a mere I£2·5m. were allocated to industrial research.[26] Though the National Council for Research and Development has more recently encouraged industrial research and development, the second set of figures quoted for a nuclear weapons programme would seem to fit the Israeli situation more adequately.

[23] *Thant Report*, p. 498.
[24] *Jerusalem Post*, 26 November, 1968.
[25] *National Science Policy and Organisation of Research in Israel*, p. 19. In Katz's opinion, 'industrial research represents a weak spot in the country's scientific effort,' *Science in Israel—1968*, p. 11.
[26] *Jewish Observer and Middle East Review* (London), 25 July, 1969, p. 16.

A significant portion of the initial capital outlay has already been invested in the construction of existing facilities, such as the Dimona reactor and its ancillary equipment, fuel processing plants and research laboratories. Nevertheless, what remains to be done before a weapon is produced will necessitate considerable expenditure. Both chemical separation and warhead assembly plants would need special equipment which would have to be either purchased abroad with foreign exchange or locally produced at great expense. Procurement abroad would be likely to betray the existence of a weapons programme.[27]

It would then be safe to conclude that, in addition to expenses incurred to date, the Israelis would have to pay between $50 and $100 million for their nuclear bombs. This would include the cost of a chemical separation plant and of weapon design and manufacture, as well as testing if it can be done in secrecy. How do these figures compare with the country's defence expenditure? The government has traditionally refrained from divulging the size of its defence budget, but this rule was broken in 1968. Published figures for the 1968-69 fiscal year put defence expenditure at I£2,200 million ($733 million), or 37 per cent of the over-all general and development budgets.[28] This marked an increase of $2\frac{1}{2}$ times over the 1966-67 budget and made Israel's defence spending the highest in the world in comparative terms.[29] In 1969-70, total defence spending was put at I£4,500 millions (21 per cent of the GNP), and Finance Minister Sapir, who released the preceding figures, announced that military expenditure during 1970-71 would take up 25 per cent of the GNP, with an initial budgetary outlay of I£3,760 millions ($1,074m.) as against I£3,300m. ($943m.) in 1969-70.[30]

To the cost of the warheads must be added that of a suitable and reliable delivery system. Israel's burden is made lighter here because she has already equipped herself with aircraft suitable for nuclear delivery as part of her conventional forces. At the same time, she has been developing a guided missile-system that could deliver small nuclear pay-loads. Annual operating costs of a 50-missile force in soft emplacement have been put at $5 million.[31]

---

[27] *New York Times*, 6 July, 1967.
[28] *Jerusalem Post*, 25 April, 1968.
[29] Brig. Yaacov Hefez, Financial Adviser to the Israeli Chief of Staff, *International Herald Tribune* (Paris), 4 April, 1969.
[30] *Jerusalem Post* (Weekly Overseas Edition), 23 February, 1970.
[31] *Thant Report*, Table 3, p. 502.

When comparing all these figures with Israel's *annual* defence spending, which even before the six-day war topped the $200 million mark, it becomes obvious that the amounts involved are not prohibitive. The likelihood that the presence of a nuclear arsenal will bring about an eventual fall-off in expenditure on conventional armaments would also play an important part in such financial calculations.

This is not to imply that cost considerations will be pushed aside by the decision-makers as lightly as the above figures might lead one to believe. As the Thant study makes abundantly clear, these amounts are only the first step on an up-hill road. Once a country develops a primitive nuclear potential, which in Israel's case would probably lead to Arab acquisition of a similar capability sooner or later, it will immediately feel the need to develop less vulnerable and more accurate delivery systems and more sophisticated and versatile nuclear warheads, in order to keep ahead in the nuclear race. Experience has demonstrated that delivery systems are responsible for the major share of the costs of a nuclear force, with the ever-present likelihood of large over-runs and continuing expensive development.

On the other hand, the fact that a sizable portion of the capital costs of warhead development have already been invested and only the reprocessing plant apparently needs to be built will operate in favour of lessening the impact of the financial burden.

CONCLUSION

The preceding review has sought to demonstrate that an Israeli nuclear weapon programme would face no insurmountable difficulties in so far as the different requirements, technical, human, financial, etc., are concerned. According to available evidence, only the final stage in plutonium production and the assembly of the device itself separate Israel from military nuclear status. Testing is not considered essential, and in this case would even be unwise, unless it can be carried out in secret. The secrecy factor is crucial for several reasons, not least among which is the easy availability of foreign uranium supplies. (The fuel problem is of particular importance and the next Chapter will be devoted to a discussion of its implications.)

In a nutshell, only the decision to go ahead with weapons development—an eminently political decision—is lacking. The possibility that it may have already been made cannot be discarded. If it has not, then whether and when such a step will be taken will depend on a combination of political, strategic and military considerations. Sheer technical capability is the insufficient but necessary condition that lends relevance to a discussion of Israel as a potential nuclear power. The foregoing analysis suggests that there is little reason to doubt the present existence of such a capability.

CHAPTER VII

The Fuel Problem

REALIZING the impact that the spread of power-producing reactors fuelled with natural uranium would have from a military point of view, given the large stockpiles of fissile material that many countries would come to possess as a by-product, the first three nuclear Powers—the United States, Britain and the Soviet Union—have developed through the years a complicated and sometimes over-lapping system of bilateral inspection agreements, guarantees, safe-guards and international organizations with the explicit objective of preventing the diversion of nuclear installations and fissile material to military uses.[1] More recently, due appreciation of the fact that, according to recent projections, by 1980 nuclear power-producing plants throughout the world will be yielding enough plutonium to build 30,000 Nagasaki-type bombs per year, and of the awesome implications for world-wide security carried by possible widespread ownership of such weapons, prompted such major international endeavours as the Non-proliferation Treaty (NPT), which was opened for signature on 1 July 1968 and became operative on 5 March 1970.

In view of this situation, were a country to embark on a weapons programme, one of its first and most urgent tasks would be to en-sure a suitable and continuing supply of control-free uranium for its reactors in the face of the many obstacles that have been created by both super-powers and the international community in general.

Safeguards have been applied in two areas: the reactor itself on the one hand, and its fuel as well as the fissile material it produces on the other. In Israel's case, only the second type concerns us, since the country that supplied the Dimona reactor—France—did not place any effective restrictions on its use. The main hurdle separat-ing Israel from virtual self-sufficiency is the acquisition of fuel with-out safeguards.

---

[1] For a brief compendium of existing control arrangements see, C. F. Barnaby, 'Existing Systems for the Control of the Peaceful Uses of Atomic Energy,' in *Preventing the Spread of Nuclear Weapons*, pp. 36-51.

What are the Israeli fuel needs? Briefly, it is calculated that some 300 to 1,000 grammes of weapons-grade plutonium can be produced from every metric ton of natural uranium burnt in a reactor. This low rate of productivity is due to the fact that the fuel cannot be left too long inside the reactor to avoid the decay of military plutonium^{239} into plutonium^{240}, whose adverse effects in some weapons designs have already been mentioned. Though plutonium^{240} has come to be assumed as a potential explosive on a par with plutonium^{239}, it remains true that a large amount of this unstable isotope would cause technical problems such as predetonation. Studies conducted by the RAND Corporation have shown that 'the attempt to use contaminated plutonium in a programme intended to produce reliable weapons of major military utility poses very serious design and testing problems. This is particularly true for ... less advanced nations with limited technological bases.'[2] It would thus be expected of countries that are inexperienced in nuclear weapons design and production to prefer as pure a grade of Pu-239 as they can obtain. This would hold true for Israel, particularly if she were planning to deploy her weapons without pre-testing. Following this line of reasoning, we may adopt the formula:

1 ton uranium 300 grammes plutonium^{329} (1)

as a sound basis for our calculations.

In plutonium-breeding reactors such as Dimona, the rate of plutonium production is about one gramme per 1,000 kilowatt-days. The Dimona reactor, with a rating of 24,000 kilowatts thermal, would, if run at full power for 300 days per year therefore produce:

$24 \times 300/1000 = 7 \cdot 2$ kilogrammes of plutonium^{239} (2)

The critical mass for atomic bombs is $5 \cdot 79$ kilogrammes of pure plutonium.[3] Israel can then produce enough plutonium at Dimona for approximately $1\frac{1}{3}$ bombs per year.

As for the natural uranium requirements, from (1) and (2):

300 grammes Pu——1 ton U
7,200 grammes Pu——7,200/300 = 24 tons U

it is deduced that Israel would need about 24 tons of uranium metal per year.[4] These rough calculations must remain approximative

[2] James R. Schlesinger, 'Nuclear Spread,' *Yale Review*, LVII (October, 1967), p. 80.
[3] Kramish, *op. cit.*, p. 21.
[4] This same figure is furnished by Beaton as the presumed annual charge of the reactor, *Must the Bomb Spread?*, p. 78.

in view of the almost total lack of published information on the Dimona facility.

The first charge of the reactor was reportedly obtained as follows: 10 tons from South Africa, 10 tons from home production from the Dead Sea phosphates, and the remaining 4 tons from French sources.[5] As shown above, a similar quantity would be required every twelve months if the reactor is used at full power in a weapons programme. How can Israel obtain 24 tons of uranium every year free of safeguards? This would seem to be the Gordian knot of the fuel problem.

Two alternative ways are open which are not mutually exclusive and will be certain to complement each other in this case. They are purchase abroad from sources not requiring safeguards as a pre-condition, and local production. Each has its pros and cons.

The latter alternative, local production as a by-product of the fertilizer industry, has one important drawback: its high cost. In 1963 it was reported that the process of production from phosphates was estimated to cost as much as ten times more per ton of uranium as the world price.[6] True, continued research since in a country endowed with resourceful scientists will have resulted in improvements that would lower this high cost, but, on the other hand, the price of uranium has also been sharply reduced from a scarcity value of $10—$12 a pound in the late 1950s to between $6 and $8 at present.[7] The main advantage of local production is that it ensures long-term self-sufficiency. This factor may be crucial in a weapons programme and it is interesting to note that a five-fold increase in the annual Israeli home production of uranium from ten tons to fifty tons was reportedly planned.[8] Even if half this expansion were

[5] *Ibid.* According to Beaton, the South African uranium was obtained through the International Atomic Energy Agency, which does not impose safeguards on transfers of up to 10 tons of natural uranium. IAEA sources indicate however that up to 31 March, 1967, only slightly more than 3 metric tons of Canadian uranium and a negligible amount of Swedish uranium had been delivered (to unspecified clients) through the Agency's supply system; O. Pedersen, 'The Supply of Nuclear Materials through the IAEA,' in *Nuclear Law for a Developing World* (Vienna: IAEA, 1969), p. 203. This does not rule out the possibility of a direct deal between Israel and South Africa.

[6] Beaton and Maddox, *op. cit.*, p. 173.

[7] See 'The Uranium Bonanza,' *The Economist* (London), 9 March, 1968, pp. 54-55.

[8] Beaton, *ibid.*, p. 79. One of the key figures in the Israel nuclear programme, physicist Amos de-Shalit (deceased on 4 September, 1969), announced on 17 October, 1968, that the new chemical complex at Arad in the Negev would produce uranium.

carried out, self-sufficiency would be attained, and Dimona could then be used free of any foreign supervision or imposed safeguards whatsoever. Since this would presumably be related to an expansion in phosphate output, the following figures should be noted:

Israel phosphate industry output

1965	350,000 tons
1967	750,000 tons
1968	1,000,000 tons
1970	1,500,000 tons (planned)[9]

Moreover, economies of scale will enter the picture at this point. A larger production of uranium will decrease the cost per ton. The importance of having an abundant fuel supply is evident also in connection with an eventual expansion of the nuclear programme, which is to be expected if the military option is taken up or if atomic power for industrial purposes is sought. That Israel will be likely to build nuclear power-plants in the near future to supplement her meagre power resources is indicated by a decision taken in April 1967 to consult the Atomic Energy Commission before any further power stations are built, 'with a view to seeing whether nuclear energy should not be used as fuel.'[10] The plutonium output of even the smallest power reactors—which must be of considerable size to be financially justifiable—would provide the country with a stockpile of considerable magnitude.

Alternatively, the procurement of uranium fuel abroad will certainly be less costly, but it is bound to face the difficulties which have been already mentioned regarding control over the fissile end-products. While some of the largest world suppliers of uranium metal have adopted export policies consonant with a non-proliferation strategy basically imposed by the super-powers, it still remains possible to obtain uranium on the market without safeguards. Confidential bilateral agreements can be concluded on a mutually profitable commercial basis which are perfectly legitimate. For some new African States, such as Gabon and the Congo, uranium exports play an important part in their struggling economies, and even South Africa emphasizes stricter controls over installations but looser

---

[9] *Jerusalem Post*, 5 September, 1968. *The Israel Economist* (Jerusalem), XXV, No. 1 (1969), p. 27.
[10] *Ibid.*, 5 April, 1967.

supervision of raw materials, and has actively sought to sell its large output of uranium in the open market. The South African attitude towards the NPT has been consistently negative. The close economic relations that exist between Israel and South Africa should be noted here. In 1966, for example, trade between these two countries amounted to I£6,737,000, which turned South Africa into Israel's most important trade partner in the African Continent.[11] The Israeli diplomatic thrust into Africa witnessed in the 1960s on the levels of development and military aid as well as cultural relations may be partly explained by a desire to secure uranium supplies. Similar efforts were deployed in Latin America, where an agreement on co-operation in the nuclear field was concluded with Brazil in December of 1967.[12]

The spread of power-producing plants using natural uranium, has resulted in a new outburst of prospecting fever. New ore fields are being discovered with frequency, and some of these finds are having great impact on the whole uranium market. The discovery of large deposits in Niger in early 1968, for example, will turn France from an important importer into a potential exporter. The net effect will be to increase the amount of uranium for purchase as well as lower its price.[13]

A third alternative which it is feared is becoming increasingly open to countries intent on acquiring a nuclear armoury, and which is essentially a short-cut to weapons production, is the acquisition of the plutonium itself. The presence of a burgeoning black market in plutonium, feeding on fissile material clandestinely diverted from peaceful programmes and otherwise unaccounted for by control bodies, has become established and has attracted the concern of the American Government. Though transactions involving nuclear materials have so far been under tight government control, as plutonium production mushrooms in the coming years and increasingly

[11] *Statistical Abstract of Israel, 1966* (Jerusalem: Central Bureau of Statistics, 1967), No. 18, p. 220.

[12] *Jerusalem Post*, 18 December, 1967.

[13] Uranium fields found in Niger, Gabon and the Central African Republic through prospecting carried out by France's Commissariat à l'Energie Atomique (CEA) will raise the annual production of French-controlled Uranium from 1270 metric tons in 1967-68 to 4300 metric tons by 1973-74 (i.e. about 10 per cent of the yearly world-wide production expected for that period). A Consortium named Uranex was formed in October 1969 to market the uranium surplus of the French nuclear programme, which is expected to amount to 2000 tons in 1973. CEA, *Notes d'Information*, October 1969, No. VI.

becomes a private, non-governmental operation, it will become progressively easier for interested customers discreetly to arrange the purchase of the fissile material for their weapon cores if they are willing to pay the right price for it. The existence of this black market is mainly due to the inadequacy of current safeguards policies and control measures and procedures to cope with the problem, as corroborated by the USAEC advisory panel specially created to study this issue.[14] It is extremely doubtful whether a greater degree of control will be possible in the future, or whether any safeguards system can be totally effective in eliminating the movement of both fissile material and uranium metal across boundaries. This applies to the NPT as well, which in Article III provides for mandatory safeguards over all fissionable material produced, processed or used by the signatory non-nuclear State 'in all nuclear activities within the territory of such State, under its jurisdiction, or carried out under its control anywhere.' Furthermore, the same Article states in its second paragraph that:

> Each State Party to the Treaty undertakes not to provide: (a) source or special fissionable material, or (b) equipment or material specially designed or prepared for the processing, use or production of special fissionable material, to any non-nuclear-weapon State for peaceful purposes, unless the source or special fissionable material shall be subject to the safeguards required by this Article.[15]

It has become evident by now that the Treaty is unlikely to be universally accepted. The countries that have shown least enthusiasm for it are precisely those 'near-nuclears' that the Treaty sponsors had primarily had in mind when drafting and negotiating the agreement. Now that the required ratifications have been obtained and the Treaty has become operative, its main impact as far as Israel's fuel procurement problems abroad are concerned will be to decrease the number of available uranium suppliers, since some of these will be signatories to the Treaty. This prospect should provide one more incentive for stepping-up local production.

[14] *New York Times*, 7 May 1967. See also 'Threat of Wayward Plutonium Worries Nuclear Institute,' *The Times*, 10 October, 1969.
[15] Source material is natural uranium; special fissionable materials are U-235, U-233 and plutonium. The safeguards required by Article III are those of the IAEA.

CHAPTER VIII

Delivery Systems

IT is a generally accepted notion that a rather sophisticated delivery system is an absolute must if a country is to possess a complete and effective nuclear strike capacity. Regardless of its destructive potential, an atomic bomb without the vehicle to deliver it to the desired target in a certain specified time is a mere 'artillery shell'. While the manufacture of the weapon itself will entail *technical* difficulties in the main, it is the delivery system that is expected to tax the *financial* resources of nations, particularly the small ones. Indeed, all studies made of the pecuniary burdens to be encountered by countries taking the nuclear road agree on assigning to the acquisition or development of an adequate means of delivery, and its maintenance and improvement, the larger share of the expenses to be incurred. Considerable sacrifices also will have to be made in terms of the scientific and industrial manpower and resources which will have to be devoted to the manufacture of the system and its maintenance. Purchase abroad will not provide an easy way out. 'Even if major components can be purchased abroad, the delivery system must be integrated into a workable whole, and this process requires the skills of a number of qualified persons, which may even exceed the number needed for warhead production.'[1]

The importance of an advanced and reliable delivery system is not limited to the mere transportation of the weapons to their targets —an offensive capability. It also has an intrinsic defensive value proportional to the degree of credibility it lends to the country's destruction potential. Credibility is essential for deterrence, and the deterrence of enemy attack is generally the main purpose of nuclear power.

An 'advanced and reliable' system today is taken to mean a missile system. This must undoubtedly be so where, firstly, geographically distant countries are concerned and, secondly, a considerable number of nuclear devices would have to be exploded to

[1] *Thant Report*, p. 501

cause crippling damage and consequently enough weapons should reach their targets. The vulnerability of aircraft and their bases to pre-emptive strikes also places a premium on missile systems, which have the advantage of easier dispersion and dissimulation.

In the Middle East, however, where the distances to be covered are not great, and where populations and industry are concentrated in small areas and a very small number of nuclear bursts would be enough to devastate the enemy, the availability of an 'assured delivery' system, i.e., of a system with a high degree of penetration capability, is not essential for credible nuclear striking-power. This same point has been made by a prominent Israeli student of nuclear strategy who formerly was Chief of Military Intelligence and was later on in charge of Strategic Research at the Ministry of Defence: 'Means of delivery are likely to constitute a lesser problem in a confrontation between small states, where relatively simple delivery vehicles may suffice.... The problem of delivery ... depends upon the distance between the country and its potential adversary and upon the adversary's means of defence.'[2]

As it has been rightly pointed out, the balance between air-defence and delivery capability is sharply tilted towards the latter in confrontations between secondary powers.[3] Big powers aside, the penetration capabilities possessed by many countries, including Israel, in the form of advanced heavy and medium bombers are considerably more sophisticated than the defence system set up against them. As a result, 'almost any country can deliver the bomb against a secondary power, even though only some countries can make the bomb.'[4]

This line or argument clearly implies that Israel does not have to develop a reliable missile system in order to possess a credible strike capability targeted against her Arab neighbours. The experience provided by the 1967 war as to the effectiveness of aircraft strikes and the extreme vulnerability of air defences under conditions of surprise attack can only reinforce this supposition. More recently, the raid carried out in September 1968 against Naj' Hammadi in Upper Egypt served to demonstrate how easy it is to penetrate Egyptian air-defences, which are virtually non-existent south

---

[2] Y. Harkabi, *Nuclear War and Nuclear Peace*, (Jerusalem: Israel Program for Scientific Translations, 1966), p. 161.
[3] Hohenemser, *op. cit.*, p. 261.
[4] *Ibid.*

of the Gulf of Suez.[5] An atomic strike against the High Dam could conceivably be carried out even by an EL AL Boeing or one of the *Noratlas* transport planes Israel possesses, particularly from bases in Sinai as this would minimize warning time. Even helicopters, which were apparently used in the 1968 raid, could deliver a warhead while flying below the reach of radar scanners, though they might need cover against point defences, including SAMs.

Notwithstanding these facts, a medium-range guided missile is being developed by the Israelis at considerable expense. In the early stages of this project, which was carried out in all secrecy, the development of a solid-fuel rocket was undertaken by the Ministry of Defence and a two-stage version, called 'Shavit-II' was tested in July 1961, which carried a sodium flare up to a height of 80 miles.[6] In October of the same year, a multi-stage version of longer range, the 'Shavit-III', was tested. At the same time, the Defence Ministry was also sponsoring intensive research in electronics, presumably with the intention of developing a guidance system, among other things. In the late 1950s studies of the upper atmosphere were already being carried out which are directly relevant to rocket and ballistic missile research.[7]

It is interesting to note in this context that the Israeli electronics industry has been rapidly developing during the last few years. An absolute yearly growth rate of 17 per cent was registered for the period 1960-66. In 1967, the net output of the industry was valued at I£75 million, 65 per cent of which went directly for national defence, and the 1969-70 output was expected to reach I£250 million. A wide range of instrumentation is being produced, including military communication equipment, radar, flight control systems, and nuclear equipment.[8]

---

[5] Israeli helicopter-borne commandos raided an Egyptian army base fifty miles west of the Suez Canal even after the introduction of improved SA-2 and sophisticated SA-3 missile systems in mid-1970, *Le Monde; Daily Telegraph* (London). 24 June, 1970.

[6] *Science* (Jerusalem: The Israel Digest, Inc., 1967), p. 35. Beaton quotes the Israel Deputy Defence Minister at the time, Shimon Peres, to the effect that the development of these rockets had been given high-priority because of 'grave defence problems', in *New Scientist* (London), 28 March, 1963.

[7] William L. Lawrence, *Science in Israel* (New York: Theodor Herzl Foundation, 1958), p. 28.

[8] See: Y. Shamir, 'The Defence Establishment as an "Aid to Progress" for the Electronic Industry,' *The Israel Economist*, XXIV, No. 10 (1968), p. 348. On the need to develop electronics to face security challenges by Israel's enemies see Shimon Peres, 'Israel's Defense in the Modern Age,' op. cit., pp. 31-34.

The local missile programme seems to have encountered some technological obstacles, possibly in connection with the development of a reliable guidance system, as evidenced by the absence of further testing—within knowledge—and by the contract entered into with the French manufacturer Marcel Dassault for the development of a medium-range guided missile.

The existence of this agreement was kept secret until it was indirectly admitted by the French government when reports circulated in January 1966 that France was to provide Israel with MRBMs were qualified to the effect that what really existed was an agreement authorizing French private firms to assist research undertaken in Israel and aimed at the production of such missiles.[9] This was an obvious face-saving formula, as in practical terms the results would be the same. Moreover, some believe the agreement went far beyond assistance to Israeli research and represented a 'welcome' contribution of Israeli capital and engineering skills to the French aerospace industry,[10] a not unlikely possibility in view of similar earlier co-operation in the atomic field.

It has since transpired that the rocket under development is a solid-fuel surface-to-surface missile, named MD-660, which has a range of about 300 miles, can be fired from a mobile ramp and carries a 1,200-pound warhead. Its range would thus cover the entire Nile valley even beyond Aswan if launched from Sinai. Its guidance system has reportedly been developed to the point of being accurate within one kilometre, with final testing conducted off the Toulon base on the Mediterranean.[11] American estimates put development costs at over $100 million.

It is certainly difficult to assess with any degree of exactitude Israel's aims in developing a missile system at such expense. In terms of cost-effectiveness, a relationship that Israelis have constantly in mind when allocating their limited resources, it is hard to justify this project outside the context of a nuclear weapons programme. One possibility, which is brought to mind by the trouble taken to obtain pinpoint accuracy, and by the reported payload, could be to assign these missiles the role of a reserve strike-capability armed with conventional warheads to be used if the air force were badly hit in a surprise attack, to which aircraft are highly vulnerable. If such were the case, the missiles could fulfil a nuclear

---

[9] *The Times*, 8 January, 1966.
[10] Hurewitz, *Middle East Politics: The Military Dimension*, p. 476.
[11] *Le Monde*, 25 April, 1968.

strike function once expanded to a point permitting them to lift the heavy primitive warheads that would be produced in the early stages, or the smaller and more sophisticated ones that would follow. A decision to manufacture nuclear weapons would therefore be probably accompanied by efforts to increase the size and power of these rockets.

No explanations of the role envisaged for this system have been given. Indeed, no mention of the missile's fate has been heard since the French embargo was imposed.[12] On the face of it, it appears that a relatively sophisticated and, in its regional context, very significant missile delivery system is being developed at the same time as a nuclear option that can be turned into a capability at short notice in such a manner as to enable Israel to put together a complete nuclear force within eighteen months to two years. Although this force would be very reduced for some time in view of the small number of warheads that can be assembled with present plutonium-producing installations, it would be sufficient to affect radically the military balance in the area.

Though these conclusions are tentative, no contradicting evidence has surfaced. The dual problem facing any delivery system is invulnerability and penetration. In a Middle Eastern context, penetration presents no particular difficulties, both because of the unsophisticated defences and the negligible warning time the short distances allow. These same factors are on the other hand responsible for the high vulnerability of aircraft systems. A small, highly mobile missile force would then provide the most adequate solution. Aircraft would still be needed for conventional strike, support and interception; therefore a combined force would be the best alternative. Moreover, in the strategic conditions following the six-day war and the occupation of the Sinai peninsula and the West Bank of the Jordan, a missile system with nuclear warheads deployed throughout Israeli-held territory would eventually provide a very credible sort of second-strike capability against an Egyptian nuclear attack. This would add a measure of stability to a future nuclear balance in the area.

Apart from her rocket work, Israel has gone a long way towards acquiring an effective aircraft delivery system as well in the process of developing a strong and modern air force for conventional warfare purposes. Under an agreement concluded in February 1966,

[12] The *International Herald Tribune* reported on 26 July, 1969 that two missiles were delivered by Dassault to the Israelis 'before a ban was imposed.'

she obtained 48 *Skyhawk* A-4E tactical bombers from the United States. By late 1970, about one hundred A-4s had been acquired. These aircraft can carry upwards of 8,000 pounds—a weight which Israeli scientists would reputedly be able to meet if they engaged in a nuclear warhead development programme[13]—and have a range of 3,000 miles with external fuel tanks added. They are excellent for roof-top flying to avoid radar-controlled defences and early detection.

On 27 December 1968, the American State Department announced the sale of 50 F-4E *Phantom II* fighter-bombers to Israel. Deliveries were started in September of 1969 and are to be completed in 1970. According to Israeli Minister Pinhas Sapir, the cost of the aircraft and their equipment would amount to $300 million.[14] Another 24 planes were purchased during 1970. The *Phantom* is considered a strategic aircraft even on a great-power scale. With a loading capacity of nine tons, and sea-level speed of 900 miles per hour, as well as Mach-2·4 speed at high altitude, it constitutes in the bomber role a delivery system against which existing defences in the Middle East offer no adequate protection.

The *Phantom* has a nuclear delivery capability and is equipped with an attitude reference and bombing computer system—known as the AN/AJB-7—designed for use in nuclear strike missions. This item was among those deleted from the aircraft supplied to Israel, in line with a generally applied policy on foreign sales,[15] but such complex equipment is not likely to constitute an essential requirement for nuclear delivery in view of the relatively unsophisticated quality of Arab defences.

While stressing the availability of advanced delivery systems, the possibility of using unorthodox means such as commercial airliners or helicopters should not be discounted. Given the proximity of the conflicting parties, the Middle East is one of the few areas where the use of such methods is feasible.

In short, if Israel develops nuclear weapons, taking them over their assigned targets will by no means be her greatest worry.

[13] Beaton and Maddox, *op. cit.*, p. 175.
[14] *Jerusalem Post*, 27 December, 1968.
[15] Raymond Hankin, 'The Phantastic Phantom,' in *Flying Review International* (London), July 1969, p. 66. According to this source, 'Israel was anxious to acquire' this bombing system.

PART III

Israel's Strategic Doctrine and Nuclear Weapons

CHAPTER IX

The Ends

WHILE the preceding pages of this study were devoted to an examination of the Israeli nuclear programme in terms of its installations, institutions and military potentialities, the focus in Part III will be on 'policy' rather than 'hardware', on the role nuclear weapons may play in the achievement of the country's objectives and on the possible strategic implications of the introduction of such weapons into the Middle East.

That a nuclear option has been actively sought by Israel on both the level of warheads and of delivery systems has been established, as has been the fact that this option is now probably ready to be exercised. What is obviously called for at this point is an examination of the State's basic security requirements and national purposes, and of the grand strategy it has developed to fulfil these requirements and achieve these purposes, so as to envisage the possible function that nuclear weapons may be assigned as a means for the execution of that strategy.

An in-depth examination of Israel's strategic doctrine would deserve, as well as require, much larger space than that alloted here. This must perforce remain a brief look at this doctrine's main tenets, particularly as stated by the Israelis themselves.

It is perhaps a truism that the fundamental strategy developed by any country is designed first and foremost to achieve basic national purposes and to secure essential needs, while taking into account the objective facts of the situation. Let us then take brief stock of these three sets of determinant factors in the Israeli situation *as they are understood by Israel's political and military leaders.*

OBJECTIVE FACTS OF THE SITUATION

The intention here is not to account for the myriad elements that fall under this heading but to point out the dominant fact in each of the political, economic and geo-demographic areas which are most likely to govern in this case the choice of strategy.

Political: The principal fact facing the Israeli leadership in the political domain is that, after more than two decades of existence,

101

their State has not been able to gain either recognition or acceptance by its neighbours, but has continued to impose itself on the area purely through the threat or use of force. The original hostility generated by its creation has consequently increased in intensity throughout the years, and has found an expression in the stated determination of the Arab world—most recently embodied in the aims of the Palestinian resistance movement—to bring about its ultimate extinction as a Zionist political entity.[1] The seriousness of the threat is increased by the fact that, in the opinion of some Israeli leaders, there exists the possibility that such 'Politicide' may degenerate into 'Genocide':

> Condemning Israel as a state has produced an inclination to condemn its people and Jews in general.... The need to substantiate the evilness of Israel has led [the Arabs] to find deeper sources in the Jews as people, their history and religion....
>
> * * *
>
> ... The trend to infer from evilness of the state the evilness of its people is of great importance, since it may cause the closure of the circle from the urge to destroy the state to the urge to exterminate its citizens, or, put in another way, the rounding off, from what I have called Politicide to Genocide.[2]

This danger of mass extinction moreover is not limited to the local Jewish population. A basic tenet of Zionist ideology is that Israel is the one and only representative of World Jewry, and on this basis her leaders claim that what is at stake in the confrontation with the Arabs is the survival of both Israel as a State and the Jews as a people. Former Premier Ben-Gurion, who not only ruled the destinies of Israel for the first decade and a half of her existence but was also mainly responsible for the strategies that were developed to face the 'Arab threat,' has made this notion quite explicit:

> And it should not be forgotten even for a moment that Israel's security problem is quite unlike that of any another country. This is no problem of borders or sovereignty, but a problem of

[1] Whether this aim is realistic or not, and whether the Arab governments have at any time since 1948 conceived of it as a viable objective or not—both debatable matters—is beside the point. It actually has been Israel's primary task to see that this goal remains practically unfeasible.

[2] Y. Harkabi, 'The Arab-Israeli Confrontation: An Israeli View,' (paper presented at the 7th Annual Conference of the Institute for Strategic Studies, London, 3 October, 1965), pp. 4 and 7.

physical survival, in the literal meaning of the word. And it is a question of the survival not only of the people of Israel but of the Jewish people the world over.[3]

Three corollaries follow from this. The first is that, considering the nature of the threat, and given the imbalance in territorial and human power potential between the two contending sides, an imbalance that can only increase with the passage of time, the only safe long-term solution for Israel is to reach a definitive peace settlement with her neighbours.

The second corollary is that, even though a settlement usually involves a compromise with sufficient concessions made by both sides to make agreement possible, given the nature of the 'declared' Arab threat Israel cannot venture to offer other than minimal concessions, which would consequently be considered unsatisfactory by the Arabs.

Israel because of its smallness enjoys very limited latitude in making concessions. Israel may suspect that any territorial concession is of importance to the Arabs if it is calculated to weaken Israel as a step towards a final onslaught.... Israel, by the nature of her position, will prefer existing dangerously, rather than offering a concession incurring the danger of nonexistence. Any concession which may weaken Israel is too big for her; for the Arabs, it is too small if it leaves the existence of Israel intact.[4]

The obvious implication here is that no freely accepted compromise is possible that may satisfy the Arabs enough to make them abandon their present intentions, which leads to the conclusion that a stalemate in regard to a mutually acceptable settlement is inevitable for as long as the ultimate objectives of either side remain unchanged. Short of such an unlikely change, the only way out of this deadlock would be the forcible imposition of a settlement by either party, an alternative contingent upon the achievement of a decisive strategic/power superiority. This can probably obtain in only two ways: through an overwhelming armed victory—a possibility exhausted and seemingly disproved by the June war—or through a

[3] David Ben-Gurion, 'Israel's Security and Her International Relations,' in Israel Government *Year Book: 1959/60* (introduction), p. 22. See also Shimon Peres, 'Jour proche et jour lointain,' *Les Temps Modernes, op. cit.*, p. 507.
[4] Harkabi, 'The Arab-Israeli Confrontation,' p. 17.

significant qualitative and quantitative improvement in military might unmatched by the opponent.

The third corollary, perhaps the most important from a strategic point of view, is that the Arab States will not agree to a definitive settlement of the conflict as long as they believe it is within their means, present or future, to do away with Israel. Israel's task, then, is to disabuse them of that idea:

> The possibility of peace between Israel and the Arab peoples depends in large measure on Israel's military strength—sufficient strength to be an effective deterrent—and on Israel's honoured position in the international arena. Only if the Arab rulers are convinced that Israel cannot be liquidated, either by military measures or by means of blockade and isolation, will they realize the need for, and the value of, peace and co-operation with Israel.[5]

In 1965 Abba Eban, the Foreign Minister, expressed himself along similar lines:

> Our policy of containment and deterrence ... has two object-ives. In the specific context of security it aims to protect our land and lives. In its political aspect, it aims to induce new currents of thought in the Arab mind. We want to create doubt—and eventually resignation and despair—about the dream of eliminating Israel from the world's map.[6]

Economic: In this sphere, the dominant fact is the scarcity of natural resources and the chronic shortage of capital. The country's dependence on the influx of financial aid from the Jewish communities abroad to balance its yearly deficit (estimated at I£1,008 million in 1970-71) and obtain essential foreign exchange is well-known. The grave recession that followed in 1965 the end of both German reparations and American foreign aid and which had attained its peak in May 1967 gives evidence of the inherent weakness of the economy. This situation posits two imperatives:

The first is to reduce as much as possible the burdens of military expenditure which the continued state of war has rendered increas-

---

[5] Ben-Gurion, *op. cit.*, p. 86.
[6] Interview by the *Jewish Observer and Middle East Review*, 2 July, 1965.

ingly heavy. Any meaningful reduction would become possible only if the state of war with the Arabs were ended.

The second is to open to Israeli industry and enterprise the only gate through which economic independence can be attained, that of regional co-operation. Wishful pronouncements notwithstanding, Israel's leaders fully realize that, for the foreseeable future, such formulated by Information Minister Israel Galili in December 1968 Arabs made largely on Israel's own terms.

Geo-Demographic: The obvious dominant factor under this heading is that Israel is a small country in surface and population surrounded by hostile neighbours and lacking in raw materials and other natural resources that could render it even partially self-sufficient. This unfavourable geographical situation is aggravated from a military point of view by the population distribution patterns—concentration in the narrow coastal area between the West Bank of the Jordan and the sea and large urban agglomerations in that area—which are imposed by the nature of the land and the location of vital resources such as water.

The security problems engendered by this situation have been constantly reflected in the country's military strategy. Of their two most important consequences the first is the belief that initiative in case of hostilities can under no circumstances be left to the Arabs. Israel must attack first if she is to have a chance of success. Pre-emptive action, notwithstanding its heavy political price, is an absolute necessity:

> Under the conditions at present obtaining, namely, the relative strength of the Israeli and Arab forces, the geostrategic characteristics of the region, and the situation in the wider sphere of international relations, ... neither side can hope to gain a decisive military victory over the other unless it adopts a strategy of surprise attack.[7]

The second is that even one military defeat is a luxury that Israel cannot afford. This General Yigal Allon has called the sense of 'no-alternative':

[7] Yigal Allon, 'The Arab-Israeli Conflict: Some Suggested Solutions,' *International Affairs* (London), XL (April, 1964), p. 209. See also Michael Howard and Robert Hunter, *Israel and the Arab World: The Crisis of 1967* Adelphi Paper No. 41 (London: The Institute for Strategic Studies, 1967), p. 29.

Either you win the war, or you will be driven into the Mediterranean—you individually and the whole nation.[8] ...

Defeat in war with the Arab States will mean no less than total destruction for Israel, and perhaps an end to the history of the Jewish people. For the Israelis, therefore, the problem of war and peace is graver than for any other nation.[9]

The smallness of the population and the ever-present consciousness of the sharp numerical imbalance between Arab and Jew have also bred an interest in averting head-on clashes except under the most favourable conditions. The Israeli Chief-of-Staff at the time of the six-day war, General Rabin, has echoed this concern:

Eight hundred and thirty dead is a high proportion of our population. Our casualties in the six-day war were higher than the proportionate total of United States casualties in the Korean and Vietnam wars put together. And this was all in six days, not 15 years.[10]

ESSENTIAL NEEDS

The two most fundamental needs of any country are to secure its continued existence, and to live and develop in peace, i.e., in conditions devoid of any major threat to its integrity. In fact, these are the two faces of a self-same coin, for continued existence is ultimately a function of constant development.

While in most other instances a country's existential continuity is measured against territorial, ethnic, or even linguistic canons, in Israel's case the continued existence of the State means the survival of its present exclusively Jewish character:

The State of Israel is a part of the Middle East only in geography, which is, in the main, a static element. From the decisive aspects of dynamism, creation and growth, Israel is a part of world Jewry. ... A community of destiny and destination joins together indissolubly the State of Israel and the Jewish people. There is an indestructible bond, a bond of life and death, between them.[11]

[8] Yigal Allon, 'The Making of Israel's Army,' in Michael Howard, ed., *The Theory and Practice of War* (London: Cassell, 1965), p. 362.
[9] Allon, 'The Arab-Israel Conflict,' p. 213.
[10] Isthak Rabin, 'Israel Appeals for Peace,' *Near East Report* (Washington, D.C.), Special Survey, May 1968, p. 12.
[11] David Ben-Gurion, *Rebirth and Destiny of Israel* (New York: Philosophical Library, 1954), p. 489.

This restrictive conception of Israel's intrinsic nature, when pitted against the homogeneity of the country's surrounding area, apparently rules out the possibility of any future large-scale regional integration. This, taken in conjunction with the bitter record of Arab-Israeli relations to date, signifies that these relations as they will eventually evolve can hardly be visualized except in terms of either Israeli dominance or submission.

But a second vital need must also be answered, the need for peace and acceptance as essential requirements for economic prosperity and long-term security. To fulfil their purposes, however, these must be accompanied by the establishment of normal relations with the neighbouring countries, primarily in the sense of commercial interchange and other forms of regional co-operation. A mere state of non-war will not do. In his introduction to the Israel Government *Year Book* of 1959-60, David Ben-Gurion defined Israel's 'crowning national goal' as

> ... True and permanent peace, and economic, cultural and political cooperation with the neighbouring countries. [These] are the supreme aims of Israel's foreign policy....[12]

Further on, he repeats the same principles:

> Since the foundation of the State (and even before), the achievement of a Jewish-Arab alliance, and political, economic and cultural co-operation between the Jews and the Arab peoples, has been the primary, principal and supreme goal of Israel's foreign policy.[13]

Yigal Allon considers 'the ultimate solution to the Arab-Israel conflict' to lie

> ... in the creation of a regional commonwealth for economic, political, scientific, cultural and security cooperation. Such a commonwealth would comprise all, or most, of the countries of the region ...[14]

This theme is ever-recurrent, and Israeli insistence on direct

[12] Ben-Gurion, 'Israel's Security,' p. 11.
[13] *Ibid.*, pp. 56-57.
[14] Allon 'The Arab-Israel Conflict,' p. 207.

negotiations and a peace treaty as the only guarantee of a meaning-ful settlement in the wake of the six-day war can be directly traced to this need to couple peace with Arab acceptance and recognition, without which there obviously can be no economic or other co-operation. Stated in unambiguous terms by Israeli leaders on many occasions since the war,[15] this determination was explicitly formulated by Information Minister Israel Galili in December 1968 in terms that remain unchanged at the time of this writing:

> The Government of Israel has not yet adopted any map con-cerning all fronts. But it has determined a major and basic prin-ciple—whereby there will be no change in the existing map that encompasses the areas stretching between the present cease-fire lines before the signing of peace treaties and the delineation of secure and recognized borders. This principle is not challenged by any member of the Cabinet.[16]

BASIC PURPOSES

Besides the obvious national purposes of economic independence, prosperity and power (influence) common to all nations, the funda-mental aim of the State of Israel is the 'ingathering of the exiles', the bringing together of the Jewish people scattered throughout the world in their 'homeland.' As Ben-Gurion put it in 1955 before the Knesset,

> It was for this that the State was established, and it is by virtue of this alone that it will stand.[17]

In an address to the Twenty-Fifth World Zionist Congress held in Jerusalem in January 1961, he stressed in the strongest terms the duty of every Jew to settle in Israel:

> ... since the day the Jewish state was established and the gates of Israel were flung open to every Jew who wanted to come, every religious Jew has daily violated the precepts of Judaism and the Torah of Israel by remaining in the Diaspora.[18]

It follows that, if Israel wishes to fulfil this basic aim of gathering

---

[15] See particularly Premier Eshkol's statement of 27 June, 1967.
[16] *Jerusalem Post* (weekly supplement), 12 December, 1968.
[17] Quoted in Israel Government, *Facts and Figures*, 1955, p. 10.
[18] Quoted in Fayez A. Sayegh, *The Arab-Israeli Conflict* (2nd ed., New York: Arab Information Center, 1964), p. 63.

in a sizeable portion of the fourteen million Jews in the world[19] while coping with her natural population increase, she has to procure space and resources suitable to this task.[20] The resulting tendency to follow an expansionist policy in search of 'lebensraum' has been provided with an ideological justification by the historical link beween the Jewish people and *Eretz Israel* (Land of Israel) that lies at the heart of Zionist theory:

> Every State consists of land and a people. Israel is no exception, but it is a State identical neither with its land nor with its people.... It must now be said that it has been established in only a portion of the Land of Israel. Even those who are dubious as to the restoration of the historical frontiers, as fixed and crystallized and given form from the beginning of time, will hardly deny the anomaly of the boundaries of the new State.[21]

This was written in 1953, and Ben-Gurion was thus expressing his dissatisfaction with the country's territorial size as it was to remain until June 1967.

It was to be expected therefore that the Israeli Government would not pursue an active peace-seeking policy for as long as the territory under its jurisdiction was insufficient for the envisaged expansion in population. This was corroborated by events up to June 1967,[22] and particularly by the Sinai campaign of 1956, one of whose 'principal

---

[19] According to the *American-Jewish Year Book*, there were approximately 13,875,000 Jews in the world at the beginning of 1970 (Vol. 71, p. 543).

[20] Speaking before the Tenth Convention of the Mapai ruling Party in February of 1965, the then Prime Minister Levi Eshkhol stated that 'by the end of the decade ... we may exhaust the reservoirs of [open] immigration from the lands of distress. But immigration from the prosperous countries, comparable in dimensions with the previous rate of immigration, will not begin all of a sudden, overnight, on the first of January 1971, unless we foster this immigration gradually during the years we have left until that date' and '... we must therefore show foresight and do all in our power to prepare the ground for immigration from the prosperous countries.' Henry M. Christman, ed., *The State Papers of Levi Eshkol* (New York: Funk and Wagnalls, 1969), pp. 44 and 35.

[21] David Ben-Gurion, 'Israel Among the Nations,' in Israel Government *Year Book: 1952*, p. 15.

[22] See Michael Ionides, *Divide and Lose: The Arab Revolt of 1955-58* (London: Geoffrey Bles, 1960); Sir John Bagot Glubb, *A Soldier With the Arabs* (London: Hodder and Stoughton, 1957); E. L. M. Burns, *Between Arab and Israeli* (London: George G. Harrap and Co., Ltd., 1962); William Bradford, *Israeli Military Strategy, 1948-1962* (unpublished dissertation).

aims' was in Ben-Gurion's own words 'the liberation of that part of the homeland which was occupied by the invaders.'[23] As a result of the six-day war, however. Israel came into possession of the whole of Palestine plus a portion of Syria valuable for its water resources and strategic position, and the entire Sinai Peninsula, rich in minerals and, as it has been recently discovered, even water.[24] This would suggest that territorial ambitions will no longer postpone serious attempts to stabilize the situation on a more or less permanent basis. In other words, Israel may have become a 'status-quo' power. Satisfaction with the post-June 1967 situation has been evinced by former Chief-of-Staff Rabin: 'From a military point of view, at least, our borders are now ideal,'[25] and by Defence Minister Moshe Dayan: 'Speaking purely theoretically, I doubt whether we could find more ideal borders than the present lines.'[26]

Thus, while the policy of the State of Israel since 1949 has been to seek to achieve with a maximum economy of force a gradual improvement of its strategic position—and of its capacity to absorb Jewish immigration—by an increase in its territory, the realization of these aims as a result of the six-day war would imply that Israel has a vested interest in the achievement, or imposition, of a settlement that would optimally give permanence to the present situation or, at least, preserve some of the strategic advantages gained in 1967.

From the above we can conclude that Israel's strategy in the post-June 1967 era is designed, firstly, to deter the Arabs from launching a war that would jeopardize the *status quo* and cost her much in terms of manpower and resources; secondly, persuade them that they cannot win a war, either now or in the future, and should therefore desist from challenging Israel's existence by violent means; and thirdly, now that optimum strategic and territorial conditions have been realized, bring about a permanent stabilization of the situation. In short, the objectives of Israeli strategy would be to

[23] Quoted in the *Jewish Observer and Middle East Review*, 16 November, 1965.

[24] Vast water resources, of about 3·5 trillion cubic feet, were discovered in March 1969 under the Sinai desert. Every year, about 35 million cubic feet of fresh water are replenished, and Israeli scientific observers have suggested that permanent settlements could be established there, *International Herald Tribune* (Paris), 9 April, 1969. See also 'Israel Discovery of Water Gives Hope to Sinai,' *The Times*, 8 April, 1969.

[25] Quoted in the *Jewish Observer and Middle East Review*, 5 January, 1968, p. 7.

[26] Quoted in Aubrey Hodes, *Dialogue With Ishmael: Israel's Future in the Middle East* (New York: Funk and Wagnalls, 1968), p. 142.

deter and persuade in the short run, and impose peace on Israel's own terms in the long run.

These objectives are not new. They are not the fruit of the altered circumstances reigning since 11 June, 1967, but have always been the stated aims of Israel's foreign and defence policies. Developments since that date have probably introduced a novel element, namely, the realization by the Israeli leadership that a maximum of expansion has been attained—at the cost of exploding the myth of Israeli inferiority which previously generated a good deal of sympathetic toleration in the West—and that the time has come for entrenchment and consolidation of the gains achieved. In other words, the imposition of 'peace' has now become the immediate goal.

If these are the aims, what should be the means? A discussion of means must be on two levels: the conventional and the nuclear.[27]

[27] By means here we refer exclusively to *military* instruments and agencies. In any conflict, *political* moves are the reflection of the parties' evaluation primarily of the balance of military power between them.

CHAPTER X

The Means: Conventional

IN January 1955, General Dayan, then in his second year as Israeli Chief of Staff, summarized the country's security problem in the following manner:

'The area of the country is only 8,100 square miles. But owing to the configuration of its territory there are 400 miles of frontier. Three-quarters of the population of Israel lives in the coastal plain, running from north of Haifa to south of Tel Aviv, with a slender salient branching off to Jerusalem. This densely settled area has an average width of no more than twelve miles between the Mediterranean and the Jordanian border. From the Israel Parliament buildings in Jerusalem the armed sentries of the Jordanian Arab Legion can be seen a few hundred yards away. The headquarters of the Israel General Staff in the coastal plain are within clear view from the hills which mark the Jordan frontier. The country's main roads and railways are exposed to swift and easy incursion. Scarcely anywhere in Israel can a man live or work beyond the easy range of enemy fire. Indeed, except in the Negev, no settlement is at a distance of more than 20 miles from an Arab frontier.'[1]

To buttress this truly handicapped position, which was further aggravated by the Arab countries' often stated determination not to accept the *fait accompli* of Israel's existence, and which was made tolerable only by the complete failure of these countries to further their aims by effective and concerted action, Israel proceeded to develop a highly efficient and modern war machine and an operational doctrine for it adapted to these geographical and political determinants.

Ever since 1948, Israel has devoted all her energies to 'the maintenance of a military force endowed with sufficient equipment and skill to deter the Arab rulers, from initiating any military action

[1] Dayan, 'Israel's Border and security Problems,' p. 250.

112

against her.[2]' No efforts, and certainly no funds, have been spared to turn the Armed Forces into a highly efficient, well-trained and adequately equipped instrument of war. Defence expenditures have always had the lion's share of the budget ($943m. in 1969-70) and yearly special budgets have also been allocated to the military effort. Manpower limitations have led to the adoption of a small, professional force as the core of the Army, which in case of emergency can within seventy-two hours be supplemented with a large reserve force of over 200,000 men. The military establishment, moreover, has been able to draw on the nation for whatever requirements it has deemed necessary for its preparedness as a matter of the highest priority, and the country as a whole has been pressed into a continuous mobilization at the service of the military forces, to the extent of branding as wasteful any effort or initiative which does not however indirectly contribute to the armed might of the state. Thus we find Ben-Gurion, for example, making the following admonition: 'Science in our days is the key ... to military strength. Our talented young people who study law, instead of science and technology, are squandering human capital, which is of inestimable value to the nation.'[3]

In short, *Zahal* (Israel Defence Forces) has been developed into a suitable instrument for the implementation of a strategy of deterrence on the one hand, and expansion whenever and wherever practicable on the other.

To be able to fulfil this double task, the Israeli Army had to become the strongest force in the arena, and its supremacy had by necessity to be beyond doubt. While deterrence implies the avoidance of battle (at least of battle initiated by the enemy), not a single challenge could be allowed to pass unanswered, since failure to respond might be interpreted as a sign of weakness and the deterrent would lose credibility. This resulted in the adoption of a strategy of instant and overwhelming retaliation for even the most minor border incidents. Implicit in this line of action was the danger of eliciting larger clashes and an accompanying general

[2] Ben-Gurion, 'Israel's Security,' pp. 79-80. On the Israeli Army see Halpern, 'The Military in Israel'; Hurewitz, 'The Role of the Military in Society and Government in Israel,' and the chapter on Israel in *Middle East Politics: The Military Dimension*; Amos Perlmutter, *Military and Politics in Israel* (New York: Praeger, 1969); Irving Heymont, 'Israeli Defence Forces,' *Military Review* (Fort Leavenworth, Kansas) February, 1967, pp. 37-47. For a summary of weapons and equipment, see the yearly issues of *The Military Balance* published by The Institute for Strategic Studies (London).

[3] Ben-Gurion, *Ibid.*, p. 24.

instability that ran against the grain of a deterrence posture aimed at discouraging any challenges to the *status quo*.

This predicament was perceptively summarized by the Egyptian editor of *Al-Ahram*, M. Hasanein Haykal shortly before the June war:

> The closure of the Gulf of Aqaba ... means first and last that the Arab nation represented by the UAR has succeeded for the first time, *vis-à-vis* Israel, in changing by force a *fait accompli* imposed on it by force ... To Israel this is the most dangerous aspect of the current situation—who can impose the accomplished fact and who possesses the power to safeguard it. Therefore it is not a matter of the Gulf of Aqaba but of something bigger. It is the whole philosophy of Israeli security. Hence I say that Israel must attack.[4]

Haykal was echoing what Israel's former Premier and master strategist, David Ben-Gurion, had said upon hearing of the Egyptian move in Aqaba, on 22 May: 'This means war. If they have closed the Straits by force, there is no alternative but to reopen them by force.'[5] This question of maintaining a credible deterrent at any cost apparently was one of the principal arguments in favour of an aggressive policy of reprisals as the most adequate manner of dealing with the problem of Arab infiltration which materialized in the early 1950s, mainly on the Jordanian and Egyptian borders. The main assumption underlying this policy instituted by the Israeli Government in 1951[6] was that the retaliatory raids—which were never commensurate with the action that elicited them but much more violent and destructive in terms of lives and property—would drive the neighbouring Arab states to clamp down on their subjects and actively seek to discourage border crossings into Israel, an assumption which was not borne out by the results. On the contrary, Israeli raids repeatedly led to counter-raids resulting in an escalation of retaliatory blows which at times seriously endangered the tenuous peace in the area. The February 1955 raid against an Egyptian military camp in the Gaza strip and 'punitive' action against the Jordanian village of Samu' in November 1966 and threats of reprisals against Syria in April 1967 actually sparked of a

---

[4] *Al Ahram* (Cairo), 26 May, 1967. Quoted in Howard and Hunter *op. cit.* p. 24.
[5] Quoted in Peres, *David's Sling*, pp. 236-37.
[6] See Fred J. Khouri, 'The Policy of Retaliation in Arab-Israeli Relations,' *Middle East Journal* (Washington, D.C.), XX (Autumn 1966), pp. 435-55.

chain of events that eventually led to the major wars of October-November 1956 and June 1967.

The Israeli insistence on following this provocative course of action—continued in the post-June 1967 period—is better understood when other, additional driving motives are taken into account. As the former Chief of Staff of UNTSO (United Nations Truce Supervisory Organization) and later of UNEF (United Nations Emergency Force) Lieutenant-General Burns has pointed out, retaliatory blows were dealt with an eye to the effect they would have on the Arab evaluation of Israel's military might, and in order to face the Arab governments squarely with their weakness and inability to put a stop to these Israeli armed forays. 'If the Egyptians did not declare war after the Gaza clash, or the Jordanians after Nahhalin, it is an indication that they and the other Arab countries were unable to defeat Israel,' stated Moshe Dayan to a meeting of Army officers in August 1955.[7] The policy of retaliation thus fell clearly within the framework of a strategy designed to deter by practical sporadic demonstrations of a preponderance of power. That this deterrent was effective was manifested on several occasions, such as President Nasser's refusal in 1964-65 to be dragged into an 'untimely war' as a result of Israel's scheme to divert a portion of the Jordan River waters to the Negev.[8]

The role assigned to the Israel Army has dictated its operational strategy: pre-emption, surprise, and indirect attack.[9]

The need to attack first so as to carry the battle away from the small and crowded Israeli territory imposed a pre-emptive strategy, and this was adopted right from the start. In the 1948 war, this strategy came to be called active defence and it consisted in robbing the enemy of the initiative, which would have enabled him 'to

[7] Quoted in E. L. M. Burns, *Between Arab and Israeli* (London: Harrap, 1962), p. 63. See Chapter 5 on 'The Israeli Policy of Retaliation' for an authoritative and particularly well-informed view. Nahhalin is a Jordanian town that was the victim of a major Israeli reprisal raid in March 1954.

[8] *New York Times*, 2 June; 5 June, 1965.

[9] The nine principles of war adopted by Zahal are: (1) maintenance of aim, (2) initiative, (3) surprise, (4) concentration, (5) economy of force, (6) protection, (7) co-operation, (8) flexibility and, (9) consciousness of purpose or cause. Allon, 'The Making of Israel's Army,' p. 371n. In addition to manpower and resource limitations, the operational requirements predicated in a basic doctrine of surprise attack undoubtedly played a principal role in the decision to establish Zahal as a unified force under a single Army Command responsible for all land, air and sea operations. [References to the Israeli 'army' thus should not be understood as including only its land component.]

choose, almost freely, the time and place for attack, and to concentrate sufficient strength to break the Jewish lines almost anywhere'.[10] This same principle remains the guiding doctrine of the Israeli army and was reiterated after the six-day war by the current Chief of Staff, General Barlev: 'The best defence is attack, and in the event of another war, the Israeli army will once more fight on enemy soil.'[11]

An offensive strategy is also called for to make possible the full use of the element of surprise, which is essential for achieving the greatest economy of force, aside from the tactical advantages it affords. Furthermore, surprise was always considered necessary in view of the well-stocked arsenal of modern armaments available to both sides, and which in terms of numbers was consistently favourable to the Arabs.[12] In the event of a major conflict, failure to tip the balance sharply in Israel's favour fairly early by exploiting the element of surprise to the full could mean a long and costly campaign which would hardly be limited to Arab territory. This situation was a source of considerable anxiety for Israeli planners because of their apprehensions regarding the negative effect that suffering a substantial number of civilian casualties would have, not only on the population's morale and staying power, but also on the prospects of future immigration and on Israel's claim to being the safest haven for Jews anywhere. Without a surprise all-out offensive that would eliminate most chances of an Arab strike, either aerial or naval, against Israeli urban centres (45 per cent of Israel's population and 80 per cent of its industry were concentrated in Haifa and

[10] *Ibid.* p. 360.
[11] Quoted in the *Jewish Observer and Middle East Review*, 5 January, 1968, p. 8. In September 1968, General Barlev repeated the Israeli determination to adopt an offensive strategy in any future war in spite of the depth achieved in June 1967: 'Principal trends in planning over the next few years in the Defence Forces depend primarily on priority. Even after the Six-Day war, we are convinced that high priorities should be given to those of our power components which have a high deterrent value and belong to the deterring forces. Those are forces capable of carrying the war to enemy territory, forces capable of defeating the enemy anywhere' (*Jerusalem Post*, 20 September, 1968).
[12] Quantitative advantage does not necessarily mean power supremacy. In fact, Western arms supply policies for the area aimed at providing Israel with a net edge over 'any combination of local Arab countries' once both quality and quantity were taken into account in regards to hardware, manpower and technological base, in the belief that this would deter Arab aggression, Geoffrey Kemp, *Arms and Security: The Egypt-Israel Case* Adelphi Paper No. 52, (London: Institute for Strategic Studies, 1968), pp. 19-20. The effects of this type of 'balance' on Israeli aggressiveness and inflexibility were apparently treated with less concern.

Tel Aviv in 1967) or that would at the very least oblige the Arab armies to fight a defensive rearguard action deep inside their territories, which would minimize the danger of their mounting raids against civilian targets in Israel, it was feared that any conflict would result in numerous civilian casualties.

Similarly, a strategy of indirect approach was the most indicated to achieve a quick victory at minimum costs. As propounded by the British strategist Liddell Hart, the true aim of strategy 'is not so much to seek battle as to seek a strategic situation so advantageous that if it does not of itself produce a decision, its continuation by a battle is sure to achieve this.'[13] In the words of the former Israeli Chief of Staff, General Yigael Yadin, 'its main object is to exploit the principles of war so fully, and in such manner, that the fate of the battle will be strategically determined before the fighting begins—or, at least, ensure that the fighting will proceed with maximum advantage to ourselves.'[14] The indirect approach thus aims at maximum dislocation of the enemy's forces prior to engagement, it includes such tactics as cutting his lines of communication, sealing off his lines of retreat, attacking him along the lines of least expectation—which would naturally be the lines of least resistance —and other diversionary tactics.

This operational strategy in all its components was used in the Sinai invasion of 1956[15] and particularly in the Six-Day war of June 1967.[16] Its effectiveness and suitability were proved beyond doubt, and the Israeli military machine satisfactorily fulfilled the activist side of its two-fold mission, namely, expansion. The absence of major Arab offensive action in the military field indicates that it also succeeded in fulfilling the passive, or deterrent, functions it was assigned. And though President Nasser's intentions in May-June 1967 will remain subject to conjecture and argument for a long time to come, it appears that the Egyptian military posture was, not to launch an offensive but to ride out the expected Israeli onslaught and then counter-attack. How much was this, as it proved, fatal strategy the fruit of political calculations—born mainly of

[13] B. H. Liddell Hart, *Strategy: The Indirect Approach* (revised edition, London: Faber and Faber, 1967), p. 339.
[14] Yigael Yadin, ' "For By Wise Counsel Thou Shalt Make Thy War",' (A Strategical Analysis of the 1948 Arab-Israeli War), Liddell Hart, *op. cit.*, Appendix II, p. 397.
[15] See Major-General Moshe Dayan, *Diary of the Sinai Campaign* (London: Weidenfeld and Nicolson, 1965), particularly the entry for 8 October, 1956.
[16] See B. H. Liddell Hart, 'Strategy of a War', *Encounter* (London), XXX (February, 1968), pp. 16-21.

international pressures plus the hope that a war might after all be averted—and how much the result of considerations mainly related to the military hazards involved in attacking 'Fortress Israel' is a moot point. It is undeniable, however, that the deterrent power of the Israeli forces was instrumental in making their opponents think twice about taking the military initiative, and thus gave the Israeli Air Force the opportunity to put in its devastating, and decisive, first strike. It is also true that in 1967 the Israeli deterrent failed in preventing a confrontation that the UAR had shunned on several previous occasions, which points to a gradual erosion of the deterrent that has become increasingly manifest since Cairo's rejection of the cease-fire in 1969 and the subsequent military build-up in Egypt.

Having attained in June 1967 the desired optimum in terms of territorial size and strategically adequate frontiers, the deterrent role of the Israel Defence Forces would then be expected to take complete ascendancy, the primary objective having become the consolidation of gains and permanent stabilization on the basis of the *status quo*.[17] The new role of Israeli military power as of June 1967 may be described as: to achieve the long-range aim of imposing peace upon the Arabs by convincing them that there is no practical alternative to acceptance of Israel's permanent existence and of the *status quo* shaped by her, and to settlement of outstanding issues through negotiations; i.e., that the use of force against Israel is, *and will remain*, a losing proposition.

In assessing the capability of their conventional military forces in the context of these post-June 1967 politico-strategic objectives, Israel's leaders will have to ask themselves the cardinal question: will conventional power truly be adequate to the task of avoiding a fourth round and imposing permanent peace?

In the immediate aftermath of the June conflict, the prevailing view was that such an overwhelming military victory was bound to bring Arab recognition and acceptance in its wake, that after three defeats the Arab States would have to reconcile themselves to the fact of Israel's permanence in their midst. The losses sustained by the Arab armies seemed to indicate that for many

[17] In April, 1968, General Barlev stated in a speech at a ceremony marking the passing out of a new batch of Zahal Officers: 'The round which we are now facing will be decisive for the Israeli people because during this round we must consolidate the gains of the Six-Day war,' adding that 'the Arab States' desire to fight us is inversely proportional to their awareness of our military potential,' (Israel Radio, 2/4/68, in the BBC *Summary of World Broadcasts*, ME/2738/A/3).

years Israel would not have to face a military threat of disquieting proportions. This view was shared by many outside observers, who tended to deny the likelihood of another round along conventional lines and to consider guerrilla warfare as the only type of conflict the Middle East would witness for the foreseeable future.[18]

The potential of guerrilla activities for fomenting unrest in the occupied territories and sapping Israeli morale can hardly be over-estimated, and the encouragement and support of sub-conventional warfare by the Arab governments in the aftermath of the June defeat was to be expected. But at the present advanced stage of the Arab-Israeli conflict, and considering the psychological trauma inflicted on the Arab world by the six-day war, it could not have been expected of the Arab governments and general staffs to rely, even for the short range, on guerrilla warfare, and assign their standing armies an inferior, or supporting strategic role, and consequently neglect their reconstruction and development into a force able to stand its ground against the Israelis. To this must be added the fact that the Palestinian resistance organizations became immediately after the six-day war—and increasingly afterwards—a strong *political* force, particularly within the countries forming the 'eastern front', as the new and 'faithful' standard-bearers of the struggle against Israel, but were to prove for varied reasons comparatively much less effective in their *military* performance against the Israelis.

Events to date seem to bear out this latter assumption. Through massive aid from the Soviet Union, the UAR by 1970 had made a fast come-back to pre-war standards quantitatively, and to an improved position qualitatively (the missile used to sink the Israeli destroyer *Eilat* is an example; another is the large number of advanced aircraft—MiG 21's and Su-7's—with which the Air Force has been equipped; the introduction of the sophisticated SA-3 anti-aircraft missile in 1970 is a third). The shock of defeat has resulted in a thorough shake-up in military training techniques and doctrine with a view to enhancing efficiency and initiative. The lessons of the last war will be assimilated, and the débacle of 1967 is unlikely to be repeated. In other words, Arab strategy since the June war has been, not to rely primarily on commando activity or on sparking off a people's war, but rapidly to recondition and rearm the military forces in order to attempt a change of the *status quo* in its favour by violent means as soon as the opportunity may present itself. In spite

[18] See for example Howard and Hunter, *op. cit.*, p. 43.

of her victory in 1967 and her accrued strategic advantages, Israel may again find herself in the near future faced by well-equipped military forces of such a standard that she will have seriously to entertain the possibility of having to fight a fourth war—which will probably be far costlier and of more uncertain outcome than the third.

In short, the chief security problem Israel's leadership will continue to face and plan for will not be Arab commando activity in the occupied territories and Israel proper but a threat emanating from a military situation similar to that obtaining in May 1967. At that time, regardless of how or who started the crisis, the Arab countries, led by the UAR, precipitated a military confrontation. Whether by miscalculation or by rashness, they were not prevented by the Israeli deterrent from taking steps that Israel had made clear would be tantamount to a declaration of war.[19] In the light of this and subsequent experience, what grounds can there be for the assurance that conventional power alone will provide a suitable deterrent in the future, especially now that, in Arab minds, the grievances of the past have been added to by the shameful defeat of the six-day war and its consequences?

Foreign guarantees may be of no avail if matters again come to a head. Even American willingness to intervene if Israel's existence becomes seriously threatened has greatly suffered in its credibility —in spite of periodic and domestically necessary US assurances— if only because the increase in the Soviet military presence in the area has led to a parallel increase in the risks of direct super-power confrontation.

If a lesson can be drawn by the Israelis from developments since the crisis of May-June 1967, and particularly from the reaction of their opponents to the defeat, it must surely be that their powerful army, even at the apex of its achievement, has failed to convince the Arabs that their only viable alternative is to acquiesce in Israel's existence and make peace with her. The prospective inability of the conventional deterrent to spare Israel a fourth round of large-scale fighting is foreshadowed in the protracted artillery and aerial war waged in 1968-70 over the Suez Canal and to a lesser degree on the eastern front. The deep-penetration air raids carried out by

<hr />

[19] Closure of the Tiran Straits to Israeli navigation, and close military co-ordination between Egypt and Jordan have been repeatedly announced by Israel to constitute a *casus belli*. This position as refers to the Straits was reiterated by Prime Minister Eshkol in his speech to the Knesset on 23 May, 1967. *Jewish Chronicle* (London), 26 May, 1967.

the Israeli Air Force near Cairo in the first months of 1970 and the unstinting efforts to retain mastery of the air over the Suez Canal zone—which brought a stronger Soviet military presence to Egypt, and a concomitant increase in her armed power, though not necessarily in her freedom of action—reflect the awareness of the Israeli leadership that the gains of 1967 cannot be retained on the strength of a passive conventional deterrent; passive deferrence would again be possible only in the wake of a political settlement acceptable to the Arabs, which would in any case divest Israel of a large proportion of the territories acquired in the six-day war. Short of a dramatic, and difficult to envisage, radical increase in the conventional military power available to Israel that would fail to be matched on the Arab side, the prospects are that the limited but very costly war—particularly in terms of lives for the manpower-handicapped Israelis—witnessed on the Suez front from mid-1969 to mid-1970 will stretch off and on indefinitely into the future, with the ever-present danger of a sudden escalation into a large-scale clash of uncertain outcome and unpredictable consequences.

This may yet prove to be a rationally unacceptable long-range option for Israel, due to already-mentioned constraints imposed by geo-demographic, economic and internal factors that have shaped the basic defensive strategy of the country since its inception. Among the admittedly restricted alternative choices open to the country's leaders, one that may eventually be considered to hold the key to ultimate security—and, perhaps, unchallenged regional supremacy—is the nuclear option that has been so painstakingly developed and carefully protected over the quarter-century of Israel's existence. A final and comprehensive political settlement of all outstanding issues between the principal contenders that would satisfy their grievances and allay their fears, thus definitely liquidating the existing conflict, cannot be counted on. Partial stop-gap political solutions, as experience indicates, will in all probability provide only a temporary easing of tension. Israel will have to continue to rely on purely military deterrence and the less effective and dependable the conventional deterrent becomes, the more relevant and adequate a strategy of nuclear deterrence may appear to be for bringing about that stabilization of the *status quo* which has become Israel's pre-eminent objective in the period of consolidation inaugurated by the conquests of the six-day war.

CHAPTER XI

The Means: Nuclear

BEFORE considering the advantages that Israel would reap from 'going nuclear' and the current factors and circumstances that may lead to the adoption of such a course of action—assuming that this has not already taken place, which is by no means certain—it would be relevant to have a brief look at the declared policy of the Israeli Government on the issue of nuclear armaments.

Declarations of Israeli officials on the specific question of nuclear weaponry and the more general issue of arms control for the Middle East region are characterized by: (1) consistency with the policy of blanket secrecy on matters connected with defence and security; (2) deliberate ambiguity within a general attitude of support in principle for control measures; and (3) studious concern for maintenance of current nuclear status indeterminate.

One of the first statements by a responsible official on Israeli intentions was made by Premier Ben-Gurion in the Knesset during the crisis brought about by the disclosure of the existence of the Dimona reactor in December 1960. He declared at that time that Dimona was intended for peaceful purposes only and that Israel had already proposed general regional disarmament to the Arab States, with mutual inspection and guarantees.[1] In June 1963 soon after the Eshkol Government replaced Ben-Gurion's, the Scientific Director of the Defence Ministry's development programme, Professor Shimon Yiftah, stated in a news conference that Israel would not erect a chemical separation plant to process the plutonium obtained at Dimona.[2] In 1965, Labour Minister Yigal Allon declared that Israel would not initiate the nuclear race in the area:

> I am aware that our efforts for the peaceful uses of nuclear power are viewed with misgivings not only by our enemies but even sometimes by our friends. I should like to take the opportunity of restating: Israel will not be the first to introduce nuclear weapons into the Middle East. May I add that Israel will not permit any of its neighbours to start this destructive race.[3]

[1] *Jerusalem Post*, 22 December, 1960.
[2] Quoted in Hodes, 'Implications of Israel's Nuclear Capability,' p. 5.
[3] *Jewish Observer and Middle East Review*, 24 December 1965.

This attitude has since been periodically reiterated by Israeli Cabinet members. Despite the apparently categorical tone of these declarations, a closer examination shows that they strictly conform to the aforementioned restrictive ground-rules. While these statements are issued normally in response to reports that Israel has the *capability* to develop nuclear weapons, they actually deny the existence of locally produced weaponry (which is not the charge) but are silent on the question of production capacity. Furthermore, the denial that *weapons* are being built, even if it were convincing in itself, clearly leaves open the possibility that nuclear explosives for 'peaceful' purposes are being developed, which can be held not to qualify as weapons until they are deployed with their delivery systems, or, alternatively, the readiness to use them against an enemy if necessary is announced by the government. As for the issue of 'introduction into the area', what the Israelis mean by this formula has never been satisfactorily clarified in any public official manner. Nuclear weapons are already present in the Middle East in the fleets of the super-powers, for instance, and a simple declaration by either the USSR or the United States could turn them into a factor in the Arab-Israeli confrontation. Alternatively, were the UAR to launch a nuclear power reactor programme giving Cairo a weapons option, it is highly unlikely that the Israelis will wait until Egypt starts exercising this option and their considerable lead time is expended before they consider that nuclear weapons have been introduced and start their own arms production. On the contrary, Israel's nuclear activities have been justified on several occasions as being in anticipation of, and as a defence against, possible nuclear acquisition by the Arab side.

Declaratory policy aside, Israel has gone steadily ahead in the development of the capacity to build atomic bombs, though the active nuclear course set by Ben-Gurion in the 1950s was ostensibly frozen by Eshkol, who appeared ready to refrain from taking the nuclear road for as long as a balance of power existed in the area and Israel had access to suitable conventional armaments.[4] In actual practice, available evidence indicates that no efforts have been spared to equip the establishment scientifically and technologically with all it would require to produce nuclear weapons at short notice.

No significant treatment of nuclear affairs and policy as regards

---

[4] Hodes, 'Implications of Israel's Nuclear Capability', Also Y.V., 'Atoms and a Middle East Tashkent', *New Outlook*, IX (March, 1966), pp. 3-7.

the Israeli programme is tolerated in the press, and public discussion of these matters is kept to a minimum. Indeed, even the Knesset is restricted in its ability to engage in debates connected with nuclear issues. Whenever the matter is raised by a member, the usual practice is for a minister to move that it be transferred to the Foreign Affairs and Security Committee, whose sessions are always held *in camera* and membership of which is in practice barred to certain political groups considered 'unreliable' by the 'security community'.[5] Such motions are invariably passed.

This restrictiveness may naturally be explained in terms of the secrecy that surrounds the nuclear establishment in particular— as is the case in most other countries—and the limitations placed on the discussion of all matters generally connected with the state's security, limitations that extend to local media and foreign correspondents alike.[6] There is however one other important reason why all nuclear matters are treated with extreme circumspection: the use made of the potential nuclear threat as an additional deterrent. As long as the true dimensions and capacity of the programme remain undisclosed, and as long as the long-term intentions of the government are not revealed, the uncertainty thus produced is expected to add a measure of caution and restraint to the movements and policies of the enemy, and lead him to overrate Israel's power.[7] The psychological element of deterrence would thereby be strengthened.

Besides its deterrent value, this deliberate ambiguity has also proved a useful factor in Israel's relations with friendly countries, particularly the United States. The nuclear capability has been used as a bargaining asset to obtain conventional weapons, such as the *Hawk* anti-aircraft missile for example.[8] As it was previously pointed out, Prime Minister Eshkol hinted on several occasions that Israel would have to exercise her nuclear option if arms of a

---

[5] A representative example of this 'community' is the group that became the 'kitchen cabinet' in the Ben-Gurion era and which Perlmutter described as composed of 'one or two favourite cabinet members, Mapai's "army specialists", several senior civil servants, Zahal's Chief of staff, the chief of intelligence, and a few selected senior officers and personal advisers,' *Military and Politics in Israel*, pp. 55-56.

[6] *New York Times*, 7 March, 1966.

[7] Beaton and Maddox, *op. cit.*, p. 177; *New York Times*, 11 November, 1968. See also pp. 38-41 above.

[8] Meyer Feldman, a former Assistant of President Kennedy, has confirmed that he had offered *Hawk* missiles to Israel in 1961 in return for an undertaking not to develop nuclear weapons; see *New York Times*, 16 June, 1968. See also Hodes, 'Implications of Israel's Nuclear Capability,' p. 6.

quality at least similar to that of the weapons supplied to her enemies were not made available to her.

Yet this policy can cut both ways, as uncertainty and suspicion may lead the UAR to strive to expand its nuclear programme and endeavour to acquire a military option in spite of the economic hardships such a decision would entail. Feeding on mutual distrust, the nuclear race, which has so far been held in abeyance through Egyptian unwillingness to engage in it, will then gather increasing momentum. As far as Egyptian ability to do so is concerned, though locally made nuclear weapons are apparently out of the question for at least seven to eight years in view of the complete absence of the required facilities, were the UAR to embark on a crash nuclear programme, this would probably lead Israel to proceed full-steam ahead with weapons development and refinement to preserve her lead, and the race would be on. This also raises the interesting possibility that Israel may one day feel constrained to 'go nuclear' simply in reaction to a UAR—or any other Arab country's—decision to resort to nuclear energy for power production, desalting, or other peaceful purposes, as such endeavours would simultaneously provide a military capability, and even undertake some sort of preventive action. This is suggested by Allon's above-quoted statement that 'Israel will not permit any of its neighbours to start this destructive [nuclear] race,' as well as by former IAEC Chairman Bergmann's dictum that 'by developing atomic energy for peaceful purposes, you reach the nuclear option. There are no two atomic energies.'[9]

It is around such nuclear-race argument that opposition to a military nuclear capability has rallied in Israel. Leadership of the movement, which is composed to a large extent of Leftist intellectuals, belongs to the Mapam Socialist party and to a 'Committee for Nuclear Disarmament of the Arab-Israeli Region.' This latter body was formed by a group of scientists, writers and public figures to press for an Israeli initiative aimed at denuclearizing the Middle East by means of a mutually supervised agreement with the Arab Governments. These 'denuclearizers' contend that Israel would have nothing to lose by suggesting such an agreement to the Arabs. If accepted, it would keep nuclear weapons out of the area—they believe that a nuclear balance would be extremely unstable—and it would also open the way to further negotiations on other issues. If rejected, the Arabs, and particularly the UAR, would have to

[9] Quoted in Leonard Beaton, 'Israel's Nuclear Policy Under Scrutiny', *The Times*, 16 January, 1969.

bear the onus of having encouraged proliferation and their prestige in the uncommitted world would suffer greatly. Moreover, Israel would then be justified in pressing ahead with nuclear development.[10]

The consistently negative[11] attitude evinced by successive Israeli Governments towards this proposal might be conceived as an indicator of their actual nuclear intentions. No adequate justification has been provided for this stance, and Foreign Minister Eban's statement, in March 1967, that 'we are not taking the initiative to form non-nuclear zones, because the Arab states will not negotiate anything with us,'[12] would indicate a rather unexpected departure from the consecrated policy of diplomatic one-upmanship that Israel has usually practised *vis-à-vis* the Arab Governments. The advantages to be derived from a diplomatic offensive along the lines suggested by the Denuclearization Committee in terms of world approbation for Israel and political embarrassment for the Arabs would, on the face of it, seem to have been passed over for no evident reason. Moreover, there was always the possibility that the Arab side would accept the proposal, in which case Israel would have achieved a breakthrough in her relations with the Arab countries that she has been seeking since 1948.

Perhaps it was the suspicion that this was precisely the one topic on which the Arabs would have been ready to negotiate that deterred the Israeli Government from putting it forward. Its reluctance even to explore the possibility of reaching a tacit mutual undertaking with Egypt to keep the area nuclear-free, and its sidetracking of the issue whenever it was raised in Parliament by insisting that Israel had always been ready to negotiate general and complete regional disarmament with the Arab Governments, seems to leave no alternative explanation. If this reading of the situation is correct, it would provide significant insights into the lengths to which the Israeli Government will go to protect the nuclear alternative from impairment.

In view of this policy record, the similarly negative attitude adopted towards the 1968 Non-Proliferation Treaty was to be expected. The main objections raised to signing the Treaty are that the

---

[10] Eliezer Livneh, 'Israel Must Come Out for Denuclearization,' *New Outlook*, IX (June, 1966), pp. 44-47; 'Keep Nuclear Weapons Out of Our Region,' (An appeal to the Israeli Knesset and Government by the Committee for Nuclear Disarmament of the Arab-Israeli Region), New Outlook, IX (July-August, 1966), pp. 64-65.
[11] *New York Times*, 7 August, 1961; 8 August, 1963.
[12] *Jerusalem Post*, 17 March, 1967.

psychological-deterrence value of the country's nuclear capacity would be surrendered, and that the guarantees against nuclear blackmail or attack provided by the super-powers through the Security Council to signatories are not adequate.[13]

The importance attached by the Americans—and the Soviets—to the success of the Treaty needs no elaboration. It is seen as a last-ditch attempt to save the world from the truly frightening possible consequences of a multiplication of independent centres of decision that are nuclear-armed and thus have the wherewithal to bring about, whether by accident, miscalculation or design, untold destruction upon opponents and third parties alike. The only convincing measure of such success must be the extent to which the near-nuclear countries—i.e., those on the threshold of weapons development—will subscribe to the Treaty. Israel being one such country, and the Middle East having gradually become an area of almost direct super-power confrontation, accession to the Treaty was bound to turn into a major negotiating asset for the Israelis. Indeed, their 'potential' nuclear weapon already has proved its effectiveness in several instances, from the *Hawk* missiles deal in 1961 to the sale of *Phantom* aircraft in December 1968, and the promise of capitalizing still further on this potential is likely to be one more compelling reason for delaying its actualization as much as possible, or at least keeping this actualization strictly secret.

Moreover, a major step such as adherence to the NPT would not only signify the relinquishment of the policy of 'deterrence through uncertainty' at a time of great crisis in Arab-Israeli relations, but would also entail a formal commitment to non-nuclear status for the foreseeable future, a step which could hardly be undone at a later date without starting a nuclear race in the region. Another important consideration is that adherence to the Treaty would by itself make it more difficult for Israel's friends, particularly the United States, to accept with equanimity an Israeli decision to produce nuclear weapons, if such a step were considered necessary sometime in the future. Such a significant concession as accession to the NPT cannot therefore be rationally expected on the part of the Israeli Government without some substantial returns to show for what amounts to a surrender—not irreversible perhaps but nevertheless real—of the obvious advantages of a nuclear

---

[13] *Jerusalem Post*, 31 May, 30 August, 21 November, 1968; *New York Times*, 20 November, 1968. For an appraisal of the Israeli position on the Treaty see Quester, *op. cit.*

option. One possible bargain the Israelis were reportedly inclined to consider is signature of the Treaty in return for a United States guarantee of secure 1967 borders.[14] Though Foreign Ministry officials have refused to comment on this subject of territorial guarantees by outside powers, when pressed on the issue of signature they have complained that Israel lacks such security guarantees against nuclear threat or attack as those enjoyed by America's European allies in NATO,[15] the clear implication being that an extension of the American nuclear umbrella to Israel would be a suitable *quid pro quo*. Washington was never likely to contemplate a step of this nature, and if only because of the obvious world-wide repercussions it would have in relation to the whole question of nuclear proliferation, not to speak of its effects on the future of America's sprawling interests in the Arab world. As far as the NPT is concerned, such an unqualified undertaking would antagonize the present subscribers to the Treaty, who have been offered only what they consider a rather doubtful guarantee through the Security Council, would deal a severe blow to the collegiate spirit in which the super-powers have been acting together on the subject of guarantees, and would raise the threshold of expectation of those near-nuclear countries that are still standing on the sidelines in hope of a better bargain probably beyond the reach— in terms of capacity and willingness—of either super-power. Since the Israelis were surely aware of such implications, the patent unrealism of their expectations places these on a par with the similarly mis-leading pronouncements in favour of mutual and complete disarmament that Israeli delegates continuously voice at international gatherings.[16]

Obviously, all these declarations, both official and otherwise, are consistent with the well-established policy of blanket security and purposeful avoidance of concrete definition as regards future plans

[14] *New York Times*, 20 November, 1968; *Davar*, 21 November, 1968; *Haaretz*, 21 November, 1968.

[15] *New York Times*, 20 November, 1968.

[16] At the 1968 Geneva Convention of Non-Nuclear States called by the United Nations to discuss the implications of the Non-Proliferation Treaty, for example, the Israeli representative stated that 'the immediate threat is from conventional rather than nuclear weapons. Consequently, the Conference should recognise the dangers to world peace and to the political and territorial integrity of States from conventional as well as nuclear weapons, and concern with the nuclear threat should not confer legitimacy by default on other means of destruction' (UN Documents, A/Conf. 35/SR, 1-20, 1 November, 1968). See also Foreign Minister Eban's speech in the Knesset, *Jerusalem Post*, 8 August, 1968.

and intentions in this particular field. They are thus designed to protect the flexibility and adaptability essential for a successful utilization of the nuclear option as a valuable bargaining tool in Israel's dealings with her sources of supply and support, particularly the United States. In this sense, the nuclear capability has already paid high dividends.

In short, while the nuclear option has been steadily developed, Israel's declared policy has been to deny any intentions of being the first to produce nuclear weapons in the area. At the same time, she has kept her atomic programme and all related matters strictly secret, in furtherance of a policy of 'deterrence through uncertainty'. In the field of nuclear arms control, she has endeavoured to retain her freedom of action regionally and internationally by refusing to take any steps that could be construed as firm indicators of her future course of action.

In the light of this brief review of declared policy and of the strategy developed to face the security problem, the crucial question comes to mind: what advantages would Israel expect to derive from possession of a nuclear capability that would lead her to reverse her stated position and go into weapons production?

It is generally agreed that countries seek nuclear power in quest of either prestige or security, or both.[17] In this case, the prestige factor would certainly be present, since a nuclear armoury would offer this small country a unique opportunity to gain an international stature that would hardly be obtainable otherwise. An Israeli bomb would eventually lead to Arab procurement of similar means, however, and prestige considerations alone can never compensate for the risks that a nuclear confrontation would entail for a country faced with such geo-strategic problems as a small territory surrounded by the enemy's, and a population concentrated in a narrow area which could be laid waste with a few bursts.

Israel would then rationally opt for nuclear status only if she felt such a step was necessary for her security; in other words, if she felt that her principal deterrent, her conventional power, had become ineffective.

As it was pointed out in the previous chapter, the Defence Forces have traditionally fulfilled a double task of deterrence—a primarily political and psychological function—and active defence-cum-expansion, a military role. Their ability to perform their

[17] See Beaton, *Must the Bomb Spread?*, Chapter 3, for a detailed treatment of incentives to proliferation. Also, Wolf Mendl, 'The Spread of Nuclear Weapons: Lessons from the Past,' in Barnaby, *op. cit.*, pp. 169-179.

'defensive' duties satisfactorily has been repeatedly proved, and there is no doubt that they can continue to protect the existence of Israel in the foreseeable future. In fact, by virtue of the sophisticated weapons purchased lately, such as the *Phantom* multi-purpose long-range aircraft, and the strategic depth acquired as a result of the last war, their defence capability is today stronger than ever before.

But the situation is not as satisfactory in regard to the long-range task of the Defence Forces: the imposition of peace in conditions favourable to the Israeli national interest, which will be accomplished only by convincing the Arabs that they must accept the existence of a strong and Zionist Israel in their midst. Not even the crushing victory of the six-day war could accomplish this feat. The basic requirement of short-term security has been assured, but the necessary conditions for the country's long-term survival and prosperity, identified by the Israelis themselves as acceptance by their Arab neighbours and eventual economic co-operation with them, today seem farther away from realization than ever. In other words, notwithstanding the victories achieved and the expansion undertaken since the creation of the State to this very day, the problem of security remains essentially unresolved. In fact, since 1967 it has become even more acute, as the dozens of Israeli casualties sustained monthly on all fronts, even within Israel proper as a result of guerrilla activity before a temporary cease-fire was imposed in 1970, patently demonstrates.[18]

This escalation is a continuing process. With the adoption by Egypt in mid-1969 of a strategy of attrition (called by Nasser exhaustion: *Istinzaf*)[19] as the course of action best suited to the

[18] A statement on the 'delicate' subject of Israeli losses was made by Defence Minister Dayan at a student meeting in Tel Aviv on 25 September, 1969, in which he revealed that 'despite the barriers, shelters, fortifications and technological devices' the monthly average of casualties to the Israeli Army (both dead and wounded) had risen in the first few months of the third year after the war to 157, compared with 80 casualties a month during the second year and 50 during the first year. Eighty per cent of the casualties were sustained on the borders and twenty per cent inland, half of them inside Israel (*Davar*, 26 September, 1969). On 5 January, 1970, Dayan disclosed in reply to a question in the Knesset that Israel had lost 113 dead and 330 wounded on the western front since April 1969, and that 73 Israelis had been killed and 525 wounded in Israel and the occupied territories since the war as a result of guerrilla activities (*International Herald Tribune*, 7 January, 1970).

[19] President Nasser announced the beginning of this new stage, which is conceived as offensive in nature, in his speech of 23 July, 1969: '... we are now embarking on the liberation operation.... We are fighting a long battle. We are prepared for a long battle to exhaust the enemy. The policy

present distribution of forces, and with the increase in the popular prestige, political leverage and extent of military operations of the resistance movements acting from bases in Jordan, Syria and, lately, Lebanon, *Zahal* has found itself gradually dragged into a vicious circle of protracted air and land warfare and across-the-border raids, partly because of its unchanged doctrine of retaliation, and partly in pure self-defence. This is not merely making any prospects of a political settlement progressively more difficult, but is also adding greatly to the already grievous burden of expenditure on defence. The serious financial problems faced at present can only render Israel proportionately more dependent on Washington's good will and less able to withstand its pressures, and as their hostile attitude to the 1969 Soviet-American talks in Washington and Four-Power meetings in New York demonstrates, for the Israelis any concession to outside pressure foreshadows a re-enactment of the 1957 Sinai withdrawal operation—which was engineered by the United States—and consequently makes them even more jittery about the security problem. The projects tabled by the Americans in December 1969 and June 1970 for a comprehensive settlement seem to confirm such fears, and it is also clear that Nasser's war of attrition is partly designed to achieve by military harassment what was attained in 1957 through political pressure.[20] Nonetheless Israel's reluctance even to consider plans based beforehand on the premise of withdrawal, however partial, does not preclude the possibility of her having to bow to Washington's will if enough pressure is exerted. But the existence of this possibility does nourish Israel's already strong desire for military self-sufficiency and cannot but add immensely to the feeling that she can only rely on herself and her power to achieve her objectives.

Sooner or later, the only logical conclusion to be drawn from developments since the six-day war, namely the failure of current methods and strategies to secure a stabilization of the present, highly favourable *status quo*, will inevitably lead to a radical reassessment and a change of approach that will be indispensable

---

of all the Arab States should be to exhaust. It is impossible for the lightning war of 5 June to be repeated. A continuous war between us and Israel exists. . . . Of course, an inevitable result, which perhaps no one can control, is the escalation of the military operations.'

[20] No doubt that internal pressures, such as military and student restiveness, and the need to restore the prestige of the regime in the wake of the 1967 defeat and give a much needed boost to the morale of the population, were also instrumental in adopting this strategy.

if the Israelis are to avoid a fourth full-scale conflict while preserving territorial gains achieved in 1967.

The retention of territories—particularly on the eastern front—would no doubt be among the most strategically important factors to be taken into account when laying down the new approach. To the openly proclaimed and already well-known historical, strategic, and political considerations that motivate the Israeli leadership must be added the more recent but not less compelling economic incentive. These territories have proved most valuable to the booming post-war Israeli economy as sources of cheap goods, services and labour, as markets for the Israeli industry and as generators of economic growth.[21] This has been recently reflected by the demands of the younger leadership—represented mainly by Dayan's Rafi party and Yigal Allon's Ahdut Haavoda group—for a closer and more rapid economic and administrative integration of the occupied areas with Israel proper, demands that were strongly resisted by the Mapai old-guard of aged, immigrant Zionists out of concern for the Jewish 'purity' of the State but which had to be finally accepted by Prime Minister Meir in mid-1969 to preserve the unity of the Labour party on the eve of the general elections.

Economic needs and security requirements have both influenced the adoption of what Dayan has euphemistically dubbed the policy of 'creating facts' in the occupied territories, which is designed to take for the time being the place of outright annexation pending direct agreement with the Arabs. This policy has been described by the Defence Minister as follows:

We have the ability to initiate changes in the basic situation, changes in structure, to a certain extent.... Of course, we should establish Jewish and Israeli possessions in the administered areas throughout, not just in the Golan, and not with the intention of withdrawing from there. These should not be tent camps which are set up and taken down. With this in mind, we should establish possession in areas from which we will not withdraw in accord with our view of the map; and it must be done. All these things— the economic ties, the human ties where people of those areas should work here and Israelis should be there, and the establishment of Jewish settlements and military bases in the areas— will eventually create a new land. It will not be the same map, the same structure, the same situation.... We must ... try to

[21] See the *Jerusalem Post* (weekly supplement), 12 December, 1968; *Quarterly Economic Review: Israel*, February 1969, pp. 5-7.

change the basic situation every day in order to make it easier for us to attain our desired goals.[22]

To sum up, in shaping the fundamental strategy of the country in the post-June 1967 era, the Israelis are faced with the need to:

1. Develop a new approach to the problem of imposing a settlement on the Arabs that would bring an end to the state of war as well as recognition and acceptance on terms compatible with Israel's national interests; and

2. Preserve the post-June 1967 territorial *status quo* or at least retain occupied territories that are of strategic importance for security while avoiding a further costly showdown.

A strategy of nuclear deterrence could seem particularly suited to this double task of convincing the Arab countries to forego their uncompromisingly hostile stance and reconcile themselves to the *status quo* without too many significant concessions in return, and the nuclear alternative is bound to come up for serious consideration. Firstly, from the military point of view, the presence of atomic weapons would conceivably go a long way towards stabilizing the existing situation, since large-scale war in their shadow would cease to be a viable alternative. Secondly, on the political front, they might be expected gradually to generate increasing pressures inside the Arab camp for a negotiated settlement that would stave off the threat of nuclear attack. On the other hand, they might set up pressures for developing counter-balancing armament while securing a Soviet nuclear guarantee for the short run; a situation of mutual nuclear deterrence would then ensue, which might not constitute an unwelcome development from the Israeli viewpoint, as will be seen.

In fact, what is being maintained here is that nuclear armament may well come to be seen by the Israelis as an appropriate and credible additional deterrent to Arab conventional military action. Credibility is not problematical in the Israeli case; it emanates from the nature itself of the enemy threat. If the ultimate aim of the Arab countries remains to eliminate Israel from the map, they could hardly hope to accomplish this in a nuclear environment without practically committing national suicide. Even the alternative and more limited goal of containing the Jewish state within its pre-June 1967 borders, which lies at the base of present Arab policy, would cease to be a rationally justifiable objective. The Israelis have

[22] In a speech to Haifa students, *Haaretz*, 2 April, 1969.

always considered their old position as highly insecure, and it would be reckless to want an insecure neighbour with hands on a nuclear trigger. The appropriateness of the nuclear deterrent would lie in the fact that, *in conjunction with the conventional power of the Israeli Army, it would effectively deny the Arabs the successful exercise of any type of armed action open to them,* and would be expected to bring about shortly their complete military immobilization.

What are the forms of armed pressure that Israel's adversaries can bring to bear against her? Allowing for slight variations and different combinations, the three basic types are: all-out war, limited border action and guerrilla warfare.

The capacity of the conventional Israeli Army to meet the threat of total conflict has already been indicated. Judging from past experience, it would be reasonable to expect the Israelis not to feel unduly alarmed at the prospects of another major round, were it not for the already indicated need to avoid large manpower losses, both civilian and military. Moreover, since this time it would be considerably more difficult to wage an offensive war, and there is no apparent need for further expansion—except perhaps in the direction of the water sources in southern Lebanon—a nuclear deterrent that would banish the possibility of major conflict and secure the latest strategically important territorial gains might be acquired on these grounds alone. These are certainly solid enough for the advocates of nuclear power in Israel to force an early decision in favour of weapons production if the balance of armaments becomes, in Israeli eyes, markedly unfavourable.

It is, however, in the more restricted but not less decisive battle being daily waged on the cease-fire lines and against the *Fedayeen* that the introduction of a nuclear capacity could play a major, though naturally indirect, role. A quick look at the post-June 1967 security situation suffices to show that the only conventional military activity the Israelis have cause to fear is localized on the Egyptian lines. It is on the Suez positions that fifty per cent of their Army casualties since 1967 have been registered, and where a loss of air mastery might permit the Egyptians to regain control of the eastern bank of the Canal and western Sinai. The guerrilla threat is restricted to the eastern front, which runs from Eilat in the south to Mount Hermon in the north and spans the Israeli borders with three countries—Jordan, Syria and Lebanon—whose armies would offer no trouble, except perhaps indirectly by aiding the *Fedayeen*, if Egypt were neutralized; these forces have always counted in the balance mainly as the potential eastern prong of a simultaneous offensive on all fronts, and not as a threat on their own.

It is to ending the grinding and morale-sapping warfare on the cease-fire lines, especially on the Egyptian front, and to the guerrilla forays which are reaching inside Israeli territory, not excluding the cities, that are addressed all the efforts of the Israeli military machine. As Chief of Staff General Barlev has made clear, the strategy of active defence as applied on the Suez front after its reactivation by Egypt was designed to 'induce the Egyptians to observe the cease-fire strictly by increasing our pressure'.[23] The obvious aim of this line of action was not only to cut Israeli losses in men and *matériel*, and turn the cease-fire lines into permanent borders through the consecration of a *fait accompli* that is no longer challenged, but also to deal a crippling blow to Arab morale by crushing any hopes of forcing Israel to retreat without the concessions inherent in a political solution. Similarly, the purpose of striking at civilian as well as military targets in Jordan and the other countries harbouring *Fedayeen* bases is primarily to drive home to the regimes and populations of these countries that the cost and sacrifices involved in their support for the resistance organizations are heavy enough to outweigh their moral commitment to the Palestinian cause and that their own interest lies in suppressing these organizations in order to avoid reprisals.[24] A deterrent effective enough to discourage the Arabs from mounting a major offensive but that is unable to check such more limited forms of warfare is obviously inadequate by itself.

The pivotal position of the UAR as the strongest military element in the Arab camp and as the cornerstone of Arab strategy *vis-à-vis* Israel is self-evident, and the virtual elimination of the Egyptian threat that the introduction of the nuclear factor could make possible would be of immense psychological as well as strategic significance. Several scenarios in which such a situation obtains could be envisaged.

A cessation of hostilities on the Suez front could be achieved

[23] *Davar*, 27 July, 1969.
[24] Y. Harkabi, *Fedayeen Action and Arab Strategy*, Adelphi Paper No. 53, (London: The Institute for Strategic Studies, December 1968), p. 24. The author states that the resistance activities are 'a challenge to the primary obligation of Israel to defend her citizens,' and that the policy of retaliation, reinstituted in 1965 a few months after *Fatah* began its incursions, was basically successful: 'the measures taken by the Jordanians against *Fatah's* marauding were motivated by these retaliatory actions and their threat.'

through a simple act of unilateral disengagement, whereby Israel would withdraw all her military forces to a distance of twenty miles from the Canal, for example, then declare the vacated band a demilitarized buffer zone, and announce her determination to answer any Egyptian attempt to cross the Canal with a nuclear strike against some predetermined targets inside the UAR.

Alternatively, the Israelis could announce a direct counter-city strategy, and threaten to bomb civilian targets such as the Arab capitals or the High Dam at Aswan if they were to find themselves engaged in a clash of disquieting proportions that might endanger their security. Though this posture may lack complete credibility because of the difficulty of delimiting with the required precision the nature and the extent of the Arab action that would trigger off a nuclear response, it is very doubtful whether a threat of this nature would be disregarded. Limited Arab action aimed at the attainment of a limited objective and recognized as such by the opponent could still be envisaged in this model. Nonetheless, since follow-up action would not be possible without courting disaster, the futility of such endeavours in terms of the over-all picture of Israeli preponderance, and the risks involved, would render them superfluous.

A third model would envisage the Israelis injecting nuclear weapons into the conflict primarily to force the super-powers to intervene. Given the acute tension reigning between Israel and the Arabs, the volatile nature of the issues dividing them, and the state of virtual war characterizing their present relations, if either side acquires a nuclear capacity, both Russia and the United States would be strongly constrained to bring their combined pressure to bear on all parties concerned in order to stabilize the situation and put limits to a conflict that would have reached the stage of seriously endangering worldwide security. This they could do only by upholding and guaranteeing the *status quo* (with perhaps some small revisions aimed at minimizing potential tension), as any attempt to introduce substantial changes into the situation might 'rock the boat' and would be fraught with precisely those grievous dangers that precipitated their intervention in the first place. The fact that the state with vested interests in the maintenance of the *status quo*, i.e., Israel, is in this case also most likely to be the nuclear parvenu would strongly militate in favour of this assumption.

It is commonly believed that the United States would look with strong disapproval upon an Israeli nuclear capacity, and might even seek to 'disengage from [its] commitments to Israel'[25] if the latter chose to exercise her option. Though it is no doubt true that an Israeli bomb might provide considerable incentives to proliferation among the undecided near-nuclear countries, and would certainly jeopardize still further the already precarious American interests in the Arab World, a clear distinction should be made between Washington's reluctance to countenance a new addition to the membership of the Nuclear Club—particularly in the Middle East—and the convenience, once proliferation has taken place, of maintaining all possible lines of communication and channels of influence open in order to remain an active factor in the new equation. It would be indeed unwise, and very unlikely, for the United States to surrender voluntarily its considerable authority in Jerusalem precisely at a time when whatever moderating influence it can exert on Israeli decision-makers might be urgently needed. Moreover, such abdication would serve no rational purpose, as the Israelis would obviously resist any attempts to divest them of their newly-acquired status once they have gone through with a public announcement of a weapons capability. One opinion holds that 'the challenge for United States policy (in such cases) will be to know when to shift from a programme of diminishing the rewards of acquiring a national nuclear weapons programme to co-operating with the fledgling nuclear power in hopes of reducing the chances of nuclear accident or war.'[26]

The situation would naturally differ if the Americans got wind of an Israeli bomb programme while the devices were still under production, or while the necessary weapons-grade plutonium was being readied in a chemical separation plant. At this 'early' stage, there would as yet be no openly announced Israeli commitment to a nuclear strategy and this would encourage the United States to exercise sufficient pressure—perhaps in the form of a cut-off in vital economic and/or military aid—to force Israel to give up her nuclear designs, open her installations to regular inspection, and subscribe to the NPT, since she would still be in a position to accept such demands without loss of face. Any envisaged military programme must therefore be expected to proceed in conditions of extreme secrecy. A weapons capability will be announced only after it has become an irreversible *fait accompli*, with which not

[25] Quester, *op. cit.*, p. 44.
[26] William B. Bader, *The United States and the Spread of Nuclear Weapons* (New York: Pegasus, for the Center of International Studies at Princeton University, 1968), p. 109.

only the Arabs but the great powers as well must learn to live.

As for the third mode of likely anti-Israeli action—guerrilla war, it has often been pointed out, with reason, that nuclear armament is largely irrelevant, both as a weapon in actual use and as a deterrent, in a guerrilla-warfare situation. The mushrooming of insurgency operations and 'wars of national liberation' in the nuclear age stands witness to the fact that atomic strikes are far from being the most suitable way to deal with a form of struggle that relies upon 'dispersion' and 'regrouping' as its main tactic and tries to achieve its aims by a gradual and shadowy process of 'erosion' against which even conventional battlefield strategy, let alone massive nuclear deterrence, has proven inadequate.

This and similar arguments are adduced by many, particularly in the Arab world, who believe that Israel will not be likely to exercise her nuclear option since it would be useless against what may become the principal future threat to her security: the long drawn-out battle against the Palestinian resistance organizations.[27] The eventual establishment of an Arab-Israeli nuclear balance, which would immobilize the conventional power of either side, would render Israel even more vulnerable to the guerrillas, since she would become less able to strike at their bases and staging areas in the Arab countries; such punitive actions might prove prohibitively risky in a nuclear environment. In other words, an Israeli bomb would provide the *Fedayeen* with the sanctuaries that are an essential requirement for a successful large-scale 'war of national liberation' and which are presently denied them by Israeli raids and airpower. In more general terms, a nuclear stalemate by its very nature encourages unconventional forms of warfare, and the guerrilla movement would burgeon in its shadow.

Though these arguments are in themselves valid, they fail to

[27] Harkabi, in *Fedayeen Action and Arab Strategy*, dismisses the guerrilla menace stating that it 'will always fall short of [its] objective of destroying Israel' (p. 34), but admits that 'sporadic subversion may become a feature in our lives for a length of time that no one can foresee' (p. 37). His analysis was completed in the autumn of 1968, however, at a time when the resistance groups were practically in the organizational phase and before they moved to the offensive in early 1969, launching the stage of 'direct confrontation'. By December, the Israelis were extending the military conscription age limit from 45 to 54 and voluntary civil defence groups were being formed in the main cities. Throughout 1969, the activities of the resistance 'by forcing local reprisal and by thus earning local sympathy, had gone far towards establishing a base for genuine guerrilla action within Israel's own jurisdiction. In military terms, this development had more significant implications for the future than any fighting on the Suez Canal' *Strategic Survey 1969* (The Institute for Strategic Studies, April 1970, p. 48).

take into consideration one basic factor that would place them in proper perspective and uncover their basic irrelevance, namely the necessarily limited role that guerrilla warfare can play in the Arab-Israeli confrontation. As even the *Fedayeen* themselves concede, their struggle cannot threaten the survival of Israel *in isolation from Arab conventional military pressure*. Their resistance is unlikely to develop into a full and self-sustaining 'People's' War of National Liberation' of the Vietnamese or even the Algerian type, due to the absence of adequate geo-demographic, strategic and political conditions. *Fatah*, for example, conceived itself in the period preceding the six-day war as a simple 'catalyst' that would by its incursions provoke Israel into armed clashes with the Arab states, which would eventually bring about a generalized Arab offensive. In the aftermath of the June defeat, the realization that victory in a conventional war could not be counted on to liberate Palestine, and the fact that over one million Palestinians were now under Israeli occupation, prompted the *Fedayeen* to adopt a long-term strategy 'composed of two elements: first, no direct confrontation ... on the military plane and second, a prolonged war—a war of attrition'.[28] Though the guerrillas now came to consider themselves as the primary instrument of anti-Israel struggle, and their type of warfare as the only means by which Zionism will be ultimately defeated, operationally they continued to rely on the Arab armies for important tactical support, such as the cover provided by Jordanian artillery for many of *Fatah*'s operations across the River Jordan. An even more significant contribution of conventional forces is the diversionary pressure they apply on the borders which prevents the Israeli Army from concentrating on counter-insurgency.[29]

Were an Israeli nuclear umbrella—or an Arab-Israeli balance of terror—to preclude Arab conventional contribution, whether direct or indirect, to the efforts of the *Fedayeen* in the field, and further allow the Israelis to devote the larger portion of their very considerable military capacities in terms of manpower, equipment and technology to fighting the irregulars, the guerrilla threat could probably be effectively neutralized with little difficulty. In fact,

[28] Hisham Sharabi, 'The Palestinian Revolutionary Struggle,' *Arab Palestinian Resistance* (published by the Palestine Liberation Army, in English), II, No. 1 (October 1969), p. 25.
[29] See Michael Hudson, 'The Palestinian Arab Resistance Movement: Its Significance in the Middle East Crisis,' *Middle East Journal*, XXIII, No. 3 (Summer 1969), p. 303.

since the different organizations operate mainly from bases in Jordan, Syria or Lebanon, and not from inside Israeli-held territory, the serious tensions which their daily border crossings are presently generating, and which often lead to armed clashes between Israel and these countries, would become too dangerous to be tolerated in a nuclear environment. Neither the Arab Governments and their populations, nor the world at large, including the great powers, could then afford to put up with or support the existence of a free, uncontrollable and purposely disruptive agent that could jeopardize at will the stability of the delicate balance inherent in nuclear deterence. A situation—which is not without precedent—might be easily envisaged where Arabs and Israelis would tacitly join forces, on either side of the borders, to suppress the guerrilla organizations and put an end to their activities.

The Palestinian Resistance has always understood and taken into account the paralyzing effect that the introduction of the nuclear factor would have on the whole spectrum of Arab military action. The Israeli effort in the atomic field was repeatedly mentioned in the early statements and appeals put out by *Fatah* in 1965 to justify its existence and the launching of its operations, which were frowned at by the Arab regimes as likely to precipitate a conflict with the Israelis for which they were not yet ready. In a typical 'Statement to Arab Journalists' in January of that year, *Fatah* explained that Israel 'needs three years of undisturbed peace to realize her strategic objectives of (1) achieving depth in population [by settling the Negev], and (2) producing an atomic deterrent.... The present phase is a decisive one in our history. We must move fast to prevent the enemy from realizing his strategic aims and turning the existing *status quo* into a permanent reality.'[30]

Occasional suggestions that the *Fedayeen* would still manage to assert themselves and, being an 'irresponsible' and desperate element, constitute a prohibitive threat in a nuclear situation by procuring themselves an atomic device, either by purchase at a supposed 'nuclear black-market' or from a China eager to have a hand in Middle Eastern affairs, can be dismissed as little more than uninformed wishful thinking. Though Peking might contemplate resorting to such unprecedented means to establish a position of influence in the Arab world—a region lying outside its direct sphere

---

[30] The text of the statement is from a pamphlet entitled *From the Fundaments of Fedayeen Action* (n.d.; n.p.), the first in a series of 'Revolutionary Studies and Experiences' published by *Fatah*.

of interests—it is difficult to imagine in what ways a nuclear-armed resistance group would serve Chinese purposes.

A NUCLEAR BALANCE?

In assessing the potential Arab reaction to an Israeli Bomb, the Israelis cannot fail to take into account the possible effects that acquisition by the Arabs themselves of similar means of mass destruction would have on their long-term security. Regardless of whatever political or military advantages would accrue from the development of a nuclear capacity, such a step will primarily depend on the degree of stability assigned to an eventual 'balance of terror' between Israel and the Arab World. And though the considerable time-lead presently possessed by the former indicates that such a situation would probably take not less than a decade to evolve, were Israel to announce a military nuclear capability elementary prudence would presumably require the Israeli leadership to assume the worst in calculating Arab changes of enlisting outside assistance to redress the balance.

For the purposes of this discussion, there is no need to speculate in detail on the means by which Egypt or any other Arab country could come into possession of a nuclear deterrent. A brief survey of possibilities shows that local production is practically out of the question for several years to come in view of the present lack of any sizable installations from which a stockpile of fissionable material may be built up. Construction of the necessary reactors, chemical separation plant and other facilities involved in the manufacture of plutonium bombs, and development of the weapons themselves, would suggest a minimum of 7-8 years for a totally indigenous programme to yield results. The only likely short-term alternative would be to obtain them from one of the nuclear powers, presumably China, or, failing that, convince either China or the Soviet Union to station a number of weapons on Arab territory while maintaining control over their use. Soviet control-free supply of nuclear arms is now precluded by the NPT, to which the Soviet Union is a depository party. Of course, there also exists the distinct possibility that, barring more substantial help, a guarantee of appropriate Soviet retaliation in case of an Israeli strike may be extended by Moscow. Something of the kind was reportedly offered to Egypt when Nasser approached the Soviet Union in December 1965 with the intention of purchasing atomic warheads.[31]

[31] *New York Times*, 4 and 21 February, 1966.

Whether it would satisfy the Arabs is problematical, and the reaction of several 'near-nuclears' to the US-Soviet offer of guarantee for signatories of the NPT indicates that such pledges which are not underwritten by a firm presence or extensive local identifiable interests do not enjoy sufficient credibility.

Theoretically, a nuclear 'balance of terror' will be stable if neither side feels an urge to launch a pre-emptive strike at the first sign of trouble, because both opponents believe they can absorb a first enemy onslaught and have enough power left to retaliate in such a manner as to inflict unacceptable damage on the adversary. This residual force has been called a 'second-strike' capability, and it has been often argued that such a capability can be ruled out on both sides in the Arab-Israeli case, partly due to the technical and financial impossibility of setting up a suitable warning and protection system in view of the short distances involved, and that consequently a regional nuclear balance would be very unstable since great advantages would accrue to the side that launched a pre-emptive attack.[32] This line of argument apparently fails to account for the all-important fact that, though a second-strike capability in its classical definition would not be available to either side, primarily because neither Israel nor the UAR can 'absorb' a nuclear attack in the accepted sense of retaining a measure of national viability, a limited capacity to strike back must certainly be envisaged simply because no first strike can be relied on to destroy *all* the nuclear weapons available to the other side. The prohibitive damage that such minimal retaliation can cause to either contender, where the bulk of the population, a large portion of industry, the political (and military) leadership and the nerve centre of administration are concentrated in one or two urban agglomerations in a narrow area, would render such first strike a suicidal proposition in any and all cases. Thus, in a situation where even a mere half-dozen bombs were available to each side, while a second-strike capacity must be ruled out, a first strike would be sheer madness. In all logic, the nuclear balance would therefore tend towards stability.

If a nuclear balance of terror is struck eventually between the Arab and Israeli camps, it would be expected of the Arabs not to concentrate their nuclear capability, in terms of bombs and/or delivery systems, in one small area or even perhaps in one country.

[32] See for example, Y. Nimrod and A. Korczyn, 'Suggested Patterns for Israeli-Egyptian Agreement to avoid Nuclear Proliferation', *New Outlook*, (Tel Aviv), January, 1967, p. 9.

This would also apply if the warheads in the Arab camp were to remain under the direct control of the nuclear power providing them. An Israeli nuclear strike would have to be large enough to destroy hostile warheads and their delivery vehicles wherever they might be dispersed over thousands of square miles in Egypt and/or Iraq, Syria and Jordan. Taking into consideration factors of accuracy, particularly if missiles are used, and penetration of Arab defences in the case of bombers, such an attack would need a far larger number of devices than Israel can be expected to possess, even in the most unlikely eventuality that destruction of all Arab atomic warheads were feasible. In other words, even an all-out Israeli strike would leave the Arabs with enough potential to deliver a riposte sufficient to destroy the fabric of Israel.

On the Arab side, a great advantage lies in the concentration of Israel's population and in the smallness of the country, and it could be argued that the detonation of a number of nuclear devices over strategically located targets might be conceived by the Arab leadership as sufficient to ensure the destruction of the weapons or means of delivery that Israel would need to mete out retaliation. Since the Arab countries may thus believe it possible to prevent an Israeli riposte, they might conceivably launch a nuclear attack at the first opportunity.

The validity of this argument might considerably strengthen the case for nuclear instability in the Middle East, were it not seriously undermined by the obvious fact that Israel does possess a suitable deterrent to such a potential threat in the form of a large Arab population, that exceeds 1,300,000 and forms the majority of the Palestinian Arabs. These are scattered throughout Israel and the territories occupied in 1967, from the Gaza Strip in the west, to Haifa and Galilee in the northern part of Israel proper, and the West Bank and Jerusalem in the east.

These territories are also strategically valuable to Israel on counts other than providing a hostage population. They would give her the opportunity to diffuse her nuclear launching sites, be they rocket platforms, silos, or airports for her bombers, and set them up close enough to the Jordan, for example, or the Suez Canal, so that if the Arab countries aimed at destroying them to prevent an Israeli riposte the cost involved in terms of Arab lives and material damage, on both sides of the borders, would by itself deter them from starting a nuclear attack.

The prospects of a stable nuclear balance were thus considerably enhanced by the Israeli expansion resulting from the six-day war.

It could be further maintained that the return of the larger part of the recently occupied territories to Arab control would not essentially invalidate some of the previous considerations. No matter who rules over the West Bank and Gaza, they will continue to contain—with Galilee and Jerusalem—the bulk of the Palestinians, apart from the fact that the Lebanese, Syrians and Jordanian areas bordering on Israel are inhabited by hundreds of thousands who certainly would not escape unscathed were a nuclear strike of obliteration launched against Israel.

It can be safely inferred from the foregoing analysis, firstly, that a nuclear balance between Israel and the Arabs would be reasonably stable, as a first strike could hardly be a rational choice from the viewpoint of both parties concerned; secondly—and this is a corollary of the first conclusion rather than a separate inference—that nuclear weaponry will be sought, whether by Israel or by any other Near Eastern country, never for the purpose of actual use but primarily with an eye to the weakening effect its presence will have on the political and psychological resistance of the opponent and his 'will to conflict'.

SUMMARY OF OPTIONS

A basic assumption underlying the foregoing analysis is that Israel will be likely to view a nuclear capability, not merely in terms of ultimate deterrence, but also as a possible instrument for the attainment of her politico-strategic objectives. On this premise, it appears that present Israeli options are the following:

A. MAINTAIN ADVANCED WEAPONS OPTION

This is probably the current situation. This strategy would imply a forsaking of the advantages of nuclear status at a time when Israeli superiority is most needed and the effectiveness of the conventional deterrent is in doubt.

1. *Accession to NPT:* Rewards would include a strengthening of the option through technological aid and plant expansion within context of 'peaceful uses'. Disadvantages are the possible weakening of deterrence effect through international inspection and negative political consequences of withdrawal from the Treaty if this step becomes necessary.
2. *No accession to NPT:* More likely alternative. Lack of universality in Treaty membership and absence of adequate super-power guarantees make posture easily tenable.

B. DEVELOP WEAPONS, NO ANNOUNCEMENT

This posture entails a renunciation of the political advantages inherent in nuclear status in terms of pressure on opponents and prestige. It might provide ultimate security in case of an overpowering surprise attack by an opponent without access to nuclear weaponry. Unless conventional military balance becomes unfavourable, a threshold capability (strategy *A*) would seem to be more advantageous as it allows for flexibility and provides bargaining leverage without risk of weapons detection.

C. DEVELOP WEAPONS, ANNOUNCE

Aim of this strategy would be to bring maximum possible pressure to bear on the Arab side so as to obtain a permanent (irreversible) settlement on most favourable terms and at minimum cost in terms of manpower. The element of ultimate deterrence would be present as well.

It would be idle to speculate whether strategy *A* or strategy *B* obtains at any particular point in time. Not only does the secrecy surrounding Israeli nuclear activities present obvious obstacles, but also the difficulty of meaningfully determining when an advanced option becomes an actual weapons capability gives very little scope for certainty in any such endeavour. By contrast, the watershed between strategies *B* and *C* is quite tangible, though the actual disclosure of a military capability can assume any of several more or less direct forms, credibility being the only requirement. In practical terms, the choice would be whether or not to move from *B* to *C*. It would be futile to attempt to predict in the absolute which may be the preferred option for Israel, since this is very much dependent on the particular set of circumstances that will prevail every time the issue is weighed by the decision-makers. The variables that are likely to affect any such decision have already been noted. What can be affirmed with reasonable confidence is that the attractiveness of strategy *C* will be directly proportional to the utility ascribed to the nuclear factor as an instrument that can effectively contribute to the realization of Israeli political and strategic objectives. This utility can become fully operative only in the measure in which the opponent becomes aware of it and moulds his behaviour accordingly.

*   *   *

ISRAEL'S STRATEGIC DOCTRINE

General André Beaufre has defined strategy as 'the art of the dialectic of two opposing wills using force to resolve their dispute'. In this clash of wills, 'a decision is achieved when a certain psychological effect has been produced on the enemy: when he becomes convinced that it is useless to start or alternatively to continue the struggle.'[33] No words could better describe the aims of Israeli strategy as it has unfolded since the establishment of the Jewish State. It is to produce this 'psychological effect', which has so far eluded them, that the Israelis may finally resort to nuclear weapons. Where conventional power has failed weapons of mass destruction would be expected to succeed in convincing the Arab populations first and their governments second of the futility of continuing their confrontation with Israel. With the realization that Israel cannot be militarily defeated, the rationale behind the permanent state of war, the economic blockade, and the policy of non-acceptance and non-recognition might be expected to break down. Moreover, whatever tendencies towards recognition and negotiations may already exist in the Arab world would be enormously strengthened. Hitherto, governments willing to negotiate had not dared to act because their position at home would have become untenable. In a nuclear context, the survival imperative might provide enough justification to make such approaches possible. Even in the more 'hostile' countries, such as the UAR and Syria, the nuclear threat might be expected to generate considerable popular pressure for a political settlement to be found to the conflict, or at least create an atmosphere in which such conciliatory gestures by the leadership would be tolerated.

This psychological impact would have a delayed-action effect, as some time would have to elapse for the significance of the radical change in the nature of the confrontation to be grasped and the necessary conclusions to be drawn.

On the operational level, however, the effects would be immediate. The fear of a nuclear strike in case of major hostilities would well-nigh eliminate the possibility of an Arab full-scale armed attack as a rational course of action. An indefinite period of 'no-war no-peace' would ensue, during which the psychologically erosive effects of the nuclear logic would be at work on the Arab will, gradually producing that pervasive feeling of 'doubt—and eventually resignation and despair—about the dream of eliminating Israel

[33] André Beaufre, *An Introduction to Strategy* (London: Faber, 1965), pp. 22-23.

from the world's map[34] that Israel's doctrine of deterrence had always sought to create. Once the possibility of military action is closed to the Arabs, they would have to come to terms with the *fait accompli* they have refused to acknowledge for over two decades

Aside from their value as guarantors of her survival, nuclear weapons could thus be conceived by Israel as an effective instrument for the attainment of the primary objectives of her foreign policy. Inasmuch as they would fulfil the same deterrent functions as the conventional forces, they would fit the requirements of Israeli strategic doctrine. Insofar as they would—by the very nature of the threat they embody—eliminate the possibility of major military conflict, they would be particularly useful for the perpetuation of a situation which, as a result of the six-day war, has become markedly favourable to Israel territorially, economically and strategically. Finally, peaceful coexistence being the only rational alternative in a nuclear context, the same factors that have operated on the East-West confrontation would be expected to affect Arab-Israeli relations, setting in motion that process of regional integration that alone can guarantee Israel's long-term security and well-being.

Is this 'nuclear approach' at all feasible? Is it credible? Is it realistic? More importantly, is it likely to induce the type of Arab reaction that would compensate for the enormous dangers all Middle East countries, including Israel, would be exposed to in a nuclear environment? Any categorical answers to these questions can only be highly arbitrary. The foregoing analysis has argued the plausibility of a nuclear strategy for Israel under certain circumstances. On the other hand, the hard-line policies that have characterized the Israeli approach to the Arab world thus far, and which are based on the premise that force is the best argument—a view that Arab leaders' pronouncements until the recent past have admittedly done little to discourage—have only succeded in fanning Arab suspicions of Israel's ultimate intentions and breeding further conflict. They have resulted in a hardening of positions and feelings that have turned the Arab-Israeli problem into the most intractable issue of our time. Would nuclear armament, the 'ultimate weapon', provide the exception to the rule and prove to be the 'ultimate pacifier' as well? It can be argued that nuclear deterrence would eventually engender *détente*, that, in Harkabi's words, 'the impossibility of war, the interlude that has occurred in the

---

[34] Abba Eban, quoted on p. 104 above.

violent embodiment of conflict, will spill over and make itself felt in a gradual easing of tension and the resolution of hostilities in other fields of conflict', and that 'deterrence is a provisional measure bringing in its train further settlements and a gradual easing of tension.... *Technology* leads to *nonwar,* and nonwar leads to peace'.[35] It is also true, however, that freezing the conflict in this fashion without at the same time attempting to acknowledge its underlying causes and seek agreeable solutions to the problems it has created would jeopardize in the long run whatever stability may be achieved through nuclear deterrence. Unless a more flexible attitude is adopted by the Israeli Government and steps are taken to meet the legitimate Palestinian grievances resulting from the enormous dislocation produced by the establishment of the Jewish State and which have gone unheeded since 1948, nuclear weapons may ensure the survival of Israel, but they can never become the true harbingers of peace.

[35] Harkabi, *Nuclear War and Nuclear Peace,* p. 253.

BIBLIOGRAPHY

Documents

Commissariat à l'Energie Atomique *Notes d'Information*. October 1969.

Israel Government Atomic Energy Commission. *Israel Research Reactor IRR-1*. A report compiled by R. S. Kahan, Rehovoth: IAEC, 1961.

Israel Government. *Facts and Figures, 1955*. Jerusalem: Government Printer, 1956.

Israel Government. *Knesset Proceedings*. Vol XXVIII (1966). Jerusalem: Government Printer, 1966.

Israel Government. *National Science Policy and Organisation of Research in Israel*. Jerusalem: Prime Minister's Office and the National Council for Research and Development, March, 1969 (revised).

Israel Government. *Statistical Abstract of Israel, 1967*. Jerusalem: Central Bureau of Statistics, 1967.

Israel Government. *Year Book: 1959/60*. Jerusalem: Government Printer, 1960.

Israel Government. *Year Book: 1960/61*. Jerusalem: Government Printer, 1961.

Israel Government. *Year Book: 1961/62*. Jerusalem: Government Printer, 1962.

Israel Government. *Year Book: 1965/66*. Jerusalem. Government Printer, 1966.

Israel Government. *Year Book: 1967/68*. Jerusalem: Government Printer, 1968.

US Arms Control and Disarmament Agency. *Documents on Disarmament, 1967*. Washington, DC: Government Printing Office, 1968.

US Atomic Energy Commission. *Annual Report to Congress, 1959*. Washington, DC: Government Printing Office, 1960.

US Atomic Energy Commission. *Annual Report to Congress, 1961*. Washington, DC: Government Printing Office, 1962.

US Atomic Energy Commission. *Annual Report to Congress, 1965*. Washington, DC: Government Printing Office, 1966.

US Congress. House. *A Bill to Authorize Participation by the United States in the Construction of a Dual-Purpose Electrical Power Generation and Desalting Plant in Israel*. HR 4307, 91st Cong., 1st sess., 1969.

US Congress. House. Desalination Plant for Israel. *Congressional Record*, 23 January, 1969, p. H431 (Daily Digest).

BIBLIOGRAPHY

US Congress. Joint Committee on Atomic Energy. *Background Material for the Review of the International Atomic Policies of the United States*, by Robert McKinney. Joint Committee Print, Vols. II and III. Washington, DC: Government Printing Office, 1960.

US Congress. Joint Committee on Atomic Energy. *Nonproliferation of Nuclear Weapons. Hearings* on S. Res. 179, 89th Cong., 2nd sess., 1966.

US Congress. Senate. Committee on Foreign Relations. *Construction of Nuclear Desalting Plants in the Middle East. Hearings* before the Committee on Foreign Relations, Senate, on S. Res. 155, 90th Cong., 1st sess., 1967.

US Congress. Senate. Committee on Foreign Relations. *War or Peace In the Middle East?* Report by Senator Joseph S. Clark on Study Mission to Greece, United Arab Republic, Jordan, and Israel. Committee Print. Washington, DC: Government Printing Office, 1967.

US Department of State. *United States Treaties and Other International Agreements*, Vol. VI, pt. 2.

US Department of State. *United States Treaties and Other International Agreements*, Vol. XVI, pt. 2.

US Department of State. *United States Treaties and Other International Agreements*, Vol. XVII, pt. 1.

United Nations. Educational Scientific and Cultural Organization. *World Directory of National Science Policy-Making Bodies*, 1968, Vol. II.

United Nations, General Assembly, *Conference of Non-Nuclear-Weapon States, Geneva, 29 August-28 September, 1968* (A/Conf. 351SR./20), 1 November, 1968.

United Nations. General Assembly. First Committee, 9th Session, *International Cooperation in Developing the Peaceful Uses of Atomic Energy: Report of the United States of America* (A/2734, A/2738, A/C.1/L.1 105), 15 November, 1954.

United Nations. Treaty Series. *Treaties and International Agreements Registered or Filed and Reported with the Secretariat of the United Nations*, Vol. 573R, No. 8320.

Books, Pamphlets and Reports

Allon, Yigal. 'The Making of Israel's Army,' *The Theory and Practice of War*. Edited by Michael Howard. London: Cassell, 1965.

Bader, William B. *The United States and the Spread of Nuclear Weapons*. New York: Pegasus, for The Centre of International Studies at Princeton University, 1968.

Bar-Zohar, Michel. *Suez—Ultra Secret*. Paris: Fayard, 1964.

——. *The Armed Prophet: a Biography of Ben-Gurion*. London: Arthur Barker, 1966.

BIBLIOGRAPHY

Barnaby, C. F., (ed.). *Preventing the Spread of Nuclear Weapons.* London: Souvenir Press for the Pugwash Movement, 1969.

Beaton, Leonard. 'Capabilities of Non-Nuclear Powers,' *A World of Nuclear Powers?* Edited by Alastair Buchan. Englewood Cliffs, NJ: Prentice-Hall Inc. for the American Assembly, Columbia University, 1966.

——. *Must the Bomb Spread?* Harmondsworth: Penguin Books in association with The Institute for Strategic Studies, 1968.

——, and Maddox, John. *The Spread of Nuclear Weapons.* London: Chatto & Windus, 1962.

Beaufre, André. *An Introduction to Strategy.* London: Faber and Faber, 1965.

Beckman, J. 'Gas Centrifuges for Cheaper Isotope Separation.' *Preventing the Spread of Nuclear Weapons.* Edited by C. F. Barnaby. London: Souvenir Press for the Pugwash Movement, 1969.

Ben-Gurion, David. *Rebirth and Destiny of Israel.* New York: Philosophical Library, 1954.

——. 'Israel Among the Nations.' Israel Government *Year Book: 1952* (introduction). Jerusalem: Government Printer, 1953.

——. 'Israel's Security and Her International Relations.' Israel Government *Year Book: 1959/60* (introduction). Jerusalem: Government Printer, 1960.

Buchan, Alastair (ed.). *A World of Nuclear Powers?* Englewood Cliffs, NJ.: Prentice-Hall Inc. for the American Assembly, 1966.

Burns, E. L. M. *Between Arab and Israeli.* London: George C. Harrap and Co., Ltd., 1962.

Christman, Henry M. (ed.). *The State Papers of Levi Eshkol.* New York: Funk and Wagnalls, 1969.

Crossmann, R. H. S. 'The Prisoner of Rehovoth.' *Chaim Weizmann: A Biography by Several Hands.* Edited by Meyer W. Weisgal and Joel Carmichael. London: Weidenfeld and Nicolson, 1962.

Dayan, Moshe. *Diary of the Sinai Campaign 1956.* London: Sphere Books Ltd., 1967.

Eisenstadt, S. N. *Israeli Society.* London: Weidenfeld and Nicolson, 1967.

Fisher, Sydney N. *The Military in the Middle East.* Columbus, Ohio: Ohio State University Press, 1963.

Ginzberg, Elie. *Report on Manpower Utilization in Israel.* Jerusalem: National Council for Research and Development, September 1961.

Glubb, Sir John Bagot. *A Soldier with the Arabs.* London: Hodder and Stoughton, 1957.

Goldschmidt, Bertrand. *The Atomic Adventure: Its Political and Technical Aspects.* English Edition. London and New York: Pergamon and Macmillan, 1964.

Halpern, Ben. 'The Military in Israel'. *The Role of the Military in Under-Developed Countries.* Edited by John J. Johnson. Princeton,

151

BIBLIOGRAPHY

NJ.: Princeton University Press, 1962.

Harkabi, Y. *Fedayeen Action and Arab Strategy*. Adelphi Paper No. 53. London: The Institute for Strategic Studies, 1968.

——. *Nuclear War and Nuclear Peace*. Jerusalem: Israel Program for Scientific Translations, 1966.

Hodes, Aubrey. *Dialogue with Ishmael: Israel's Future in the Middle East*. New York: Funk & Wagnalls, 1968.

Hoehn, W. E. *The Economics of Nuclear Reactors for Power and Desalting*, RM-5227-PR/ISA. Santa Monica, Calif.: Rand Corporation, 1967.

Hohenemser, Christoph. 'The Nth Country Problem Today.' *Disarmament: Its Politics and Economics*. Edited by Seymour Melman. Boston: The American Academy of Arts and Sciences, 1962.

Howard, Michael (ed.). *The Theory and Practice of War*. London: Cassell, 1965.

——, and Hunter, Robert. *Israel and the Arab World: The Crisis of 1967*. Adelphi Paper No. 41, London: The Institute for Strategic Studies, 1967.

Hurewitz, J. C. *Middle East Politics: The Military Dimension*. New York: Praeger for the Council on Foreign Relations, 1969.

——. 'The Role of the Military in Society and Government in Israel.' *The Military in the Middle East*. Edited by Sydney N. Fisher. Columbus, Ohio: Ohio State University Press, 1963.

Institute for Strategic Studies. *Strategic Survey 1969*. London: April 1970.

International Atomic Energy Agency. *Nuclear Law for a Developing World*, Lectures given at a Training Course, Vienna, 18-26 April, 1968. Vienna: IAEA, 1969.

——. *Small and Medium-Size Power Reactors*. Proceedings of a Panel, Vienna, 24-28 June, 1968. Vienna: IAEA, 1969.

Ionides, Michael. *Divide and Lose: The Arab Revolt of 1955-58*. London: Geoffrey Bles, 1960.

Israel Atomic Energy Commission. *Israel Research Reactor IRR-1*, a Report compiled by R. S. Kahan. Rehovoth: IAEC, 1961.

Johnson, John J. *The Role of the Military in Under-Developed Countries*. Princeton, NJ.: Princeton University Press, 1962.

Kaiser Engineers of Oakland, Cal., and Catalytic Construction Company of Philadelphia, Penn. *Engineering Feasibility and Economic Study for Dual-Purpose Electric-Power Desalting Plant for Israel*. Prepared for the United States-Israel Joint Board, n.p., January 1966.

Katz, Shaul. *Science in Israel 1968*. Jerusalem: Publications Service of the Prime Minister's Office, 1968.

Kemp, Geoffrey. *Arms and Security: The Egypt-Israel Case*. Adelphi Paper No. 52. London: The Institute for Strategic Studies, 1968.

Kramish, Arnold. *The Peaceful Atom in Foreign Policy*. New York:

BIBLIOGRAPHY

Harper & Row for the Council on Foreign Relations, 1963.

Laurence, William L. *Science in Israel.* New York: Theodor Herzl Foundation, 1958.

Liddell Hart, Basil H. *Strategy: The Indirect Approach.* Revised edition, London: Faber and Faber, 1967.

Melman, Seymour. *Disarmament: Its Politics and Economics.* Boston: The American Academy of Arts and Sciences, 1962.

Mendl, Wolf. 'The Spread of Nuclear Weapons: Lessons from the Past.' *Preventing the Spread of Nuclear Weapons.* Edited by C. F. Barnaby. London: Souvenir Press for the Pugwash Movement, 1969.

Nelken, M. 'Electric Power in Israel,' in IAEA, *Small and Medium-Size Power Reactors* (Proceedings of a Panel, Vienna, 24-28 June, 1968). Vienna: IAEA, 1969.

Oak Ridge National Laboratory. *Nuclear Energy Centers, Industrial and Agro-Industrial Complexes.* ORNL-4290, UC-80-Reactor Technology. Oak Ridge, Tenn.: ORNL, November, 1968.

Palestine Liberation Movement. (Fatah–Harakat at-Tahrir al-Filastiniyah). *From the Fundaments of Fida'iyin Action.* (arabic) n.p., August 1967.

Pedersen, O. 'The Supply of Nuclear Materials through the IAEA.' in *Nuclear Law for a Developing World.* Lectures given at a Training Course, Vienna, 18-26 April, 1968. Vienna: IAEA, 1969.

Peres, Shimon. *David's Sling.* London: Weidenfeld and Nicolson, 1970.

Perlmutter, Amos. *Military and Politics in Israel.* New York: Praeger, 1969.

Sayegh, Fayez A. *The Arab-Israeli Conflict.* 2nd ed. New York: Arab Information Center, 1964.

Scheinman, Lawrence. *Atomic Energy Policy in France Under the Fourth Republic.* Princeton, NJ.: Princeton University Press, 1965.

Science. Jerusalem: The Israel Digest, Inc., 1967.

Tauber, Gerald. *Scientific Endeavor of Israel.* New York: Herzl Press, 1961.

Wechsberg, Joseph. *A Walk through the Garden of Science: A Profile of the Weizmann Institute.* London: Weidenfeld and Nicolson, 1967.

Weisgal, Meyer W., and Carmichael, Joel (eds.). *Chaim Weizmann: A Biography by Several Hands.* London: Weidenfeld and Nicolson, 1962.

Weizmann, Chaim. *Trial and Error.* London: East and West Library, 1950.

Weizmann Institute of Science. *Scientific Activities 1967.* Rehovoth, 1968.

Weizmann, Vera and Tutaev, David. *The Impossible Takes Longer.* London: Hamish Hamilton, 1967.

BIBLIOGRAPHY

Wolfowitz, P. *Middle East Nuclear Desalting: Economic and Political Considerations,* RM-6019-FF. Santa Monica, Calif.: Rand Corporation, 1969.

'A World of Nuclear Powers?' *Report of the International Assembly on Nuclear Weapons, 23-26 June, 1966.* Toronto, Canada.

Yadin, Yigael. 'For By Wise Counsel Thou Shalt Make Thy War,' in *Strategy: The Indirect Approach,* by B. H. Liddell Hart. London: Faber and Faber, 1967.

Zahlan, Antoine. *Science and Higher Education in Israel.* Beirut: The Institute for Palestine Studies, 1970.

Articles

Allon, Yigal. 'The Arab-Israeli Conflict: Some Suggested Solutions.' *International Affairs* (London), XL (April 1964).

Beaton, Leonard, 'Nuclear Fuel-for-All.' *Foreign Affairs* (New York), XLV (July 1967).

——. 'Israel's Nuclear Policy under Scrutiny.' *The Times* (London), 16 January, 1969.

——. 'Why Israel Does not Need the Bomb.' *New Middle East* (London), April 1969.

Bohn, Lewis C. 'Atoms for Peace and Atoms for War.' *Disarmament and Arms Control* (Oxford), III (Spring 1965).

Clawson, Marion; Landsberg, Hans H.; and Alexander, Lyle T. 'Desalted Seawater for Agriculture: Is It Economic?' *Science* (Washington, DC), 6 June, 1969.

Dayan, Moshe, 'Israel's Border and Security Problem.' *Foreign Affairs,* XXXIII (January, 1955).

Dlayahu, E. 'Economic Considerations in Introducing Desalted Water into Agriculture.' *Value to Agriculture of High-Quality Water from Nuclear Desalination.* Vienna: International Atomic Energy Agency, 1969.

Eban, Abba. Interview. *Jewish Observer and Middle East Review* (London), 2 July, 1965.

Eisenhower, Dwight D. 'A Proposal for Our Time.' *Reader's Digest* (New York), June, 1968.

Eytan, Walter. Interview. *Nucleonics* (New York), October, 1955.

Hankin, Raymond. 'The Phantastic Phantom.' *Flying Review International* (London), July, 1969.

Heymont, Irving. 'Israeli Defence Forces,' *Military Review* (Fort Leavenworth, Kansas), February, 1969.

Hodes, Aubrey. 'Implications of Israel's Nuclear Capability.' *The Wiener Library Bulletin* (London), XXII (Autumn, 1968).

Hudson, Michael. 'The Palestinian Arab Resistance Movement: Its Significance in the Middle East Crisis.' *Middle East Journal* (Washington, DC), XXIII, No. 3 (Summer 1969).

BIBLIOGRAPHY

Katzenbach, Nicholas deB. 'The Nuclear Nonproliferation Treaty—A Vital Step In Bringing the Atom Under Control.' US Department of State. *Bulletin*, 20 May, 1968.

'Keep Nuclear Weapons Out of Our Region.' Appeal by the Committee for Nuclear Disarmament of the Arab-Israeli Region. *New Outlook* (Tel Aviv), IX (July-August, 1966).

Khouri, Fred J. 'The Policy of Retaliation in Arab-Israeli Relations.' *Middle East Journal*, XX (Autumn, 1966).

Leach, Gerald, and Wilson, Andrew. 'Will Wilson Let the Germans Share Secrets of "Volksbomb"?' *Observer* (London), 9 February, 1969.

Liddell Hart, Basil H. 'Strategy of a War.' *Encounter* (London), XXX (February, 1968).

Livneh, Eliezer. 'Israel Must Come Out for Denuclearization.' *New Outlook*, IX (June, 1966).

Nimrod, Yoram. 'L'eau, L'atome et le conflit.' *Les Temps Modernes* (Paris), XXII, No. 253Bis (1967).

Pelah, Israel. 'The Israeli Atomic Research Reactor and its Uses.' *Madda* (Tel Aviv), February 1961, (in Hebrew).

Peres, Shimon. 'Jour proche et jour lointain.' *Les Temps Modernes*, XXII, No. 253Bis (1967).

——. 'Israel's Defence in the Modern Age,' *Israel Year Book, 1965* (Tel Aviv), n.d.

Perlmutter, Amos. 'The Institutionalisation of Civil-Military Relations In Israel: The Ben-Gurion Legacy and its Challengers.' *Middle East Journal*, XXII, No. 4 (Autumn, 1968).

——. 'The Israeli Army in Politics: The Persistence of the Civilian over the Military.' *World Politics* (Princeton, New Jersey), XX, No. 4 (July, 1962).

Quester, George. 'Israel and the Non-Proliferation Treaty.' *Bulletin of the Atomic Scientists* (Chicago), XXV (June, 1969).

Rabin, Isthak. 'Israel Appeals for Peace.' *Near East Report* (Washington, DC), Special Survey, May, 1968.

Schlesinger, James R. 'Nuclear Spread.' *Yale Review* (New Haven, Conn.), LVII (October, 1967).

Shamir, Y. 'The Defense Establishment as an "Aid to Progress" for the Electronic Industry.' *Israel Economist* (Jerusalem), October, 1968.

Sharabi, Hisham. 'The Palestinian Revolutionary Struggle.' *Arab Palestinian Resistance* (Damascus), II, No. 1 (October, 1969).

Smith, Hedrick, 'US Assumes the Israelis Have A-Bomb or Its Parts', *New York Times*, 18 July, 1970.

'The Uranium Bonanza.' *Economist* (London), 9 March, 1968.

V., Y. 'Atoms and a Middle East Tashkent.' *New Outlook*, IX (March, 1966).

Zarhi, Shaul. 'Peace and the Israeli Economy.' *New Outlook*, IX (February, 1966).

BIBLIOGRAPHY

Newspapers and Other Periodicals
Articles derived from periodical sources are included in the entries under *Articles*.
Business Week (New York)
Flying Review International (London)
Haboker (Tel Aviv)
International Herald Tribune (Paris)
Interavia (Geneva)
Israel Digest (Jerusalem)
Israel Economist (Jerusalem)
Jerusalem Post (Jerusalem)
Jewish Chronicle (London)
Jewish Observer and Middle East Review (London)
Jewish Telegraphic Agency Daily News Bulletin (New York)
Le Monde (Paris)
New York Times (New York)
Quarterly Economic Review: Israel (London)
The Sunday Times (London)
The Times (London)
Washington Post (Washington, DC).

Unpublished Material
Bradford, William. 'Israeli Military Strategy, 1948-1962.' Unpublished dissertation, n.d.
Harkabi, Y. 'The Arab-Israeli Confrontation: An Israeli View.' Paper presented at the 7th Annual Conference of The Institute for Strategic Studies, London, 3 October, 1965.
Lane, J. A. 'US Studies on Agro-Industrial Complexes.' Paper presented at the International Survey Course on Economic and Technical Aspects of Nuclear Power, IAEA, Vienna, 1-12 September, 1969.

Radio Broadcasts
Bergmann, Ernst David. *Kol Yisrael* (Voice of Israel), 19 November, 1954. Foreign Broadcast Information Service *Daily Report*, 23 November, 1954.
Barlev, Gen. Haim. *Kol Yisrael* (Voice of Israel), 2 April, 1968. British Broadcasting Corporation *Summary of World Broadcasts*, ME/2738/A/3.

INDEX

INDEX

159

INDEX

Israel Electrical Corporation, 57
Israeli Engineers Association, 83
Israel Institute of Technology, see Technion
Israel Management Institute, 83

Japan, and nuclear fuel production, 73
Jerusalem, 144
Jordan, Arab Legion, 112; desalinisation plants in, 62; guerrilla activity, 114, 140; and Israeli retaliation, 135; and West Bank status, 144; passim, 131, 134, 143, 144
Jordan River, Israeli diversion scheme, 115
Johnson, Lyndon B., and American aid to Israel, 58-9; and Dimona, 48-9
June War, 1967, 103-4, 109, 110, 114-15; Israeli strategy in, 117-18; results of, 118-21

Kaiser Feasibility Study, 56 n., 58-60
Katchalski, Ephraim, 51, 83
Kennedy, John F., and Dimona, 36
Knesset, 126; nuclear development secrecy, 35, 124

Latin America, 91
Lavon, Pinhas, 27
'Lavon Affair', 55
Lebanon, 131, 134, 144; and guerrilla activity, 140
Liddell Hart, B. H., and role of strategy, 117

Manpower Resources, 46 f.
Mapai Party, 132; and divisions of, 28; and Ministry of Defense, 55
Mapam Party, 125
MD-660 surface-to-surface missile, 96
Mediterranean Sea, 96
Medium Range Ballistic Missile (MRBM), 96
Meir, Golda, 132; and crisis with US, 1957, 35
Military Strategy, deterrence and secrecy of, 36; also see Israel; strategy and Strategy
Middle East Study Group, and agro-industrial development, 63
MiG-21 interceptor, 119
Ministerial Security Committee, 55
Missile system, cost, 84, 85; development of, 81, 84, 85, 95, 96-7; production of, 94-7
Moch, Jules, 20

Mount Hermon, 134

Nagasaki, 28
Nahal Soreq reactor, 25 f.; and American aid for, 29; and capacity of, 29; and Defence, Ministry of, 19, 30, 51; and International Atomic Energy Agency, 30; and military role of, 31-2; and safety guarantees, 30; Research Centre, and nuclear development, 44; and research Facilities, 43
Nahhalin (Jordan), 115
Naj Hamadi, 94
Nasser, Gamel Abdel, and France, 27; and Jordon River diversion scheme, 115; and June War strategy, 117; and Soviet nuclear deterrence, 141; and war of attrition, 130, 131
National Council for Research and Development, functions of, 49 ff., 83
NATO, see North Atlantic Treaty Organisation
Negev, 112, 140; and Jordan River diversion scheme, 115; uranium deposits in, 15, 17
Negev Institute for Arid Zone Research, 49
Negev Nuclear Centre, 43
Netherlands, nuclear fuel production, 73
New York Times, and Dimona, 38-9
Niger, uranium discoveries in, 91
Nixon, Richard M., and Arab-Israeli conflict, 60; and nuclear desalinasation, 60
Non-Proliferation Treaty, 9, 137; importance of, 126-28; and Israel, 61, 126-8, 144, 145-6; and international nuclear co-operation, 87; and South Africa, 91; and Soviet-American guarantees, 142; and Soviet nuclear aid to Arab states, 141; and supply of fissionable materials, 92; and the US, 127
Noratlas transport plane, and nuclear delivery system, 95
North Alantic Treaty Organisation, 128
Norway, heavy water production, 17, 20
Nuclear devices, see Fuses
Nuclear energy, 9, 15, 57 f.; and desalinisation, 56-7; development of, 15-68; and dual purpose plants, 62; and electricity production, 56; feasibility of, 64; reactors, 65-6; also see Dimona, Nahal Soreq

162

INDEX

Nuclear installations, and international inspection, 87; and military significance, 25-55

Nuclear Test Ban Treaty, 80

Nuclear Weapons capability, and Arab Israeli conflict, 37-41; and Arab reaction, 141-4; and arms race, 125-6, 127; and costs of development, 82-5; and the decision making process, 52-4; and delivery system of, 84, 93-8; and Dimona, 36; and Israeli foreign relations, 81, 126-9; and fuel problem of, 87-92; and guerrilla warfare, 138-41; and Mapai Party, 28; and Ministry of Defense, 50 f.; plant and research facilities for, 42 f.; public debate about, 53; safeguard restrictions of, 87; and secrecy about, 27; and strike force, 97; testing, 79-81; warhead assembly plant, 84

Oak Ridge Institute of Nuclear Studies, and Israeli students, 26

Oak Ridge National Laboratory, and desalinisation, 62, 63; and agro-industrial nuclear centres, 63

Palestine, 110, 139; resistance organisations, 102, 119; also see Arab-Israeli conflict, Fatah, Fedayeen

Patterson, Morehead, 25

Peres, Shimon, as Ben-Gurion 'Hawk', 27; and Israeli nuclear capability, 26, 40-1, 48; Perrin, F., 21; Phantom II aircraft, 127, 130; deliveries to Israel, 98; and nuclear delivery, 98

Perrin, François, 21

Phantom aircraft, 127, 130

Phosphates, and uranium production, 15, 89-90

Plutonium, 9; black market in, 91; and chemical separation process, 76-7; and Dimona Centre, 78, 80-1, 88; and nuclear policy, 49; and Reprocessing Plant, 49; procurement of, 77-8; production of, 65-6, 75-8, 85, 87, 88-92, 97, 137

Pre-emption, 115-16

Rabin, Isthak, and June War, 110

Racah, Professor, 16

Radar, and nuclear delivery system, 95

Rafi Party, 132

Rand Corporation and nuclear fuel research, 88

Reactors, Nuclear, 65-6; also see Dimona; Nahal Soreq

Rocketry, research and development, 27, 95-6

Safeguard System, Nuclear, and bilateral agreements, 66; and black market in fissionable material, 91, 92; and international inspection, 36, 38, 64, 87

Samburski, Professor, 18

Samu, 114

Sapir, Pinhas, and arms expenditure, 98

Scientific education, 46 f.

Scientific Research Council, 49

Seaborg, Glenn, 77

Sharett, Moshe, and defense policies, 27; as Prime Minister, 20

Shavit II, 95

Shavit III, 95

Sieff Institute, 46

Sinai, 134; Israel withdrawal from, 1957, 131; occupation of, 110; and war, 1957, 109

Skyhawk A-4 aircraft, deliveries to Israel, 97-8; and nuclear delivery capability of, 98

Socialism, tradition of, 28

South Africa, trade with Israel, 91; uranium exports, 90-1

Soviet-American Talks, 1969, 131

Soviet Union, aid to UAR, 37, 119, 120; and Arab-Israeli conflict, 123; and Arab nuclear co-operation, 37, 141; and international inspection, 87; nuclear deterrence of, 20, 123; and Non-Proliferation Treaty, 127

Strategy, Israeli, 110-21, 129-48; Arab, 130-44

Suez Canal, 120, 134

Suez, Gulf of, 94

Sukhoi Su-7 Fitter aircraft, 119

Surface-to-surface missiles, 95-6

Syria, 131, 134, 143, 144; and guerrilla activity, 140; and occupied territory, 110

Tal, Eliezer, 50

Tahal, and Israeli water resources, 56

Technion Institute, 23; and nuclear development, 44-6

Tel Aviv, 112

Testing, Nuclear, 79-81

Toulon (France), 96

Thant Report, 47 n.

Trombay (India),, 78

Tzour, Michael, 83

INDEX

JABBER: Israel and nuclear weapons

WI

WITHDRAWN